"This is a much-needed practical guide for all seeking to be Spirit-filled, leading th
recommend th
blessed as I w is
time to drink d er,
Townsville, Aus

IF YOU ARE THIRSTY YOU CAN BE SPIRIT-FILLED

BE EMPOWERED FOR LIFE AND WITNESS

PETER ROENNFELDT

SIGNS PUBLISHING®
Established 1885

"*If You Are Thirsty, You Can Be Spirit-filled* is refreshing, empowering and transformational. Peter brings clarity to the role of the Holy Spirit and what it means to live a Spirit-filled life. In a time when people are crying out for Living Water, this book speaks powerfully to our church."—Alina and Martin van Rensburg, young adult ministry leaders, Brisbane, Australia

"Finally, a practical book that unpacks the dynamic of the Holy Spirit for our lives and the God-centred journey we all dream of. Peter Roennfeldt provides a rich mix of theological depth and practical application for the most under-capitalised engine room of our faith—a life filled with the Spirit of God."—Dr Nick Kross, youth specialist, South Pacific Discipleship Ministry Team, Sydney

"Until recently I've not placed much emphasis on Holy Spirit baptism and Paul's command that all believers baptised by immersion 'need to be continually filled by the Holy Spirit' (Ephesians 5:18, as in the original). During my own personal revival in experiencing the Spirit's daily filling, Peter Roennfeldt sent me his book, in which he applies the biblical narrative for Spirit baptism and daily filling to our great need—individually and as a church."
—Terry Johnson, pastor and denominational leader, Sydney, Australia

Dedication

To all who thirst for the Holy Spirit's filling.

Proudly published and printed in Australia by
Signs Publishing
Warburton, Victoria.

This book was
Edited by Lauren Webb and Nathan Brown
Proofread by Nathan Brown and Lauren Webb
Cover design by Shane Winfield
Cover image by Visual Art by Gajic/istockphoto.com
Typeset in Berkeley Book 11/14 pt

ISBN (print edition) 978 1 922373 18 2
ISBN (ebook edition) 978 1 922373 19 9

CONTENTS

WATER: A PRIORITY

It was a struggle for families to survive on the heavily forested blocks of land allocated to Australian World War II ex-servicemen. There were no amenities, houses or sheds, let alone fences or clearings for growing fruit trees or vegetables or grazing livestock.

During most of my childhood and early teen years, my dad leased McLeod's farm—a small property in the southwest of Western Australia. We used this farm as a base to work the war-service blocks allocated to him, fencing and clearing the land by hand.

Australia is the world's driest inhabited continent, and we were very conscious of the importance of water. We humans need lots of water and can only survive a short time without it. Water is essential for life.

My childhood pre-dates concerns about global warming and climate change, but we knew the devastation of drought and ravaging bushfires. Consequently, when a property was being considered for farming, the question of adequate water for home and cattle was a priority. Were there streams or rivers on the property? And did they flow all year? Was there underground water? What was the condition of the dams, wells, water tanks, windmills and pumps? Would there be an adequate supply of water to survive without rain if there was drought?

There were a number of streams on McLeod's farm. A stony creek bed crossed Caves Road to the east, which was then fed from a spring on the hillside below our house. Another stream flowed from near the dam on the hill opposite, another from the tea-trees behind the dairy, and another stream flowed from the swamps at the back of McLeod's house. When it rained, the flow of each stream increased substantially.

The streams were all different. Some tumbled over rocks and others moved quietly among the rushes, some were brackish from the swamps they passed through and others were crystal clear. However, the various streams on the farm converged and flowed along a valley, on the edge of what we called "the long paddock"—ultimately flowing into the Margaret River.

In this book, we will explore the streams of the Holy Spirit's presence in our lives. When these converge, the Spirit quenches our deepest spiritual thirst, revitalising our lives and empowering our witness for Jesus.

The Holy Spirit quenches our deepest spiritual thirst, revitalising our lives and empowering our witness for Jesus.

If you are thirsty

Physical thirst signals dehydration. Having endured the extreme temperatures and physical exertion of walking through the wilderness and along the rugged paths of Galilee, Judea and Samaria, Jesus understood thirst. He also identified with the social and spiritual thirst of those He met along the way—their desperate longing for love, care, compassion, healing, peace and justice.

Today, *thirst* has become urban slang for excessive attention-seeking.[1] Used like this, thirst conveys the idea of acting in a manner that "encroaches on boundaries and intrudes on others' space, jostling self-respect and good taste out of the way."[2] In her *New York Times* essay, Carina Chocano observed that this type of thirst is "a condition that exists on a very wide spectrum." She noted, "The guy who eagerly favourites your every social [media] post is thirsty. The co-worker who's always fishing for the boss's praise is thirsty. The brand that tries very hard to be cool is thirsty."[3] You can probably think of other examples—politicians, athletes and entertainment stars. Many are thirsty.

But whether someone is thirsty for healing, wholeness, goodness and love, or for attention, praise, success and material gain, the only water that can truly quench this thirst is *living water*.

The Spirit quenches thirst

Jesus first spoke of living water with a Samaritan woman at Jacob's well, 50 kilometres (about 30 miles) north of Jerusalem. Jesus' disciples had gone into town to buy food, while He had stayed by the well. It was midday and the sun was high in the sky when the woman came to draw water. She was shocked when Jesus asked her for a drink, for Jews and Samaritans did not speak—and being a woman was another social barrier.

Jesus ignored her reaction and went straight to the point, "If you knew the gift of God and who it is that asks you for a drink, you would have asked him and he would have given you living water" (John 4:10, NIV).

The woman missed the magnitude of Jesus' offer, pointing out that He didn't have anything to draw water with and dismissing the idea that His water could be better than that from the well of their ancestor Jacob. He responded to her scepticism by telling her, "Everyone who drinks this water will be thirsty again, but whoever drinks the water I give them will never thirst. Indeed, the water I give them will become in them a spring of water welling up to eternal life" (John 4:13, 14, NIV).

Jesus saw the thirst of this broken woman and offered to quench it. When introducing His apostles to the crowds on the Galilean hills a few months later, He said, "Blessed are those who hunger and thirst for righteousness, for they will be filled" (Matthew 5:6, NIV). And, when visiting in Jerusalem later in His ministry, it became clear that the Spirit was the living water who could quench her thirst (see John 7:37–39).

The Spirit revitalises life

In recent years, Australia has experienced widespread drought. Farmers have suffered terribly, their livelihoods stripped from them. We've seen millions of square kilometres of the country burn in devasting bushfires, with enormous loss of lives, homes, infrastructure, livestock and wildlife. Footage of koalas begging for water, blackened forests and heavy choking smoke blanketing the country and cities was broadcast around the globe and led to an outpouring of support.

When rain falls, it is always a cause for celebration. While it is still coming down in torrents, kids—and adults too—are out splashing in the rain, and watching wild birds and animals negotiating the swollen streams and rushing waters. In the towns and cities, people open their doors and windows, neighbours connect with each other and communities come alive.

In the same way, the showers of the Spirit refresh, rejuvenate and renew life—revitalising us, our families, friends, colleagues and communities. And while rain can be unreliable, the Spirit's presence can be counted on.

The Spirit empowers witness

The second time Jesus spoke of living water was in Jerusalem's temple courts about six months before His crucifixion. He was again speaking to thirsty people.

On the final day of the festival of *Sukkot*—also called the Feast of Shelters or Tabernacles—crowds gathered at the temple to watch the ceremonies. Jesus stood up in the midst of the people and shouted: "Anyone who is thirsty may come to me! Anyone who believes in me may come and drink! For the Scriptures declare, 'Rivers of living water will flow from his heart'" (John 7:37, 38).

John explains that the living water Jesus invited the people to drink was the Spirit, who would quench the thirst of believers. The Spirit would then flow from their hearts into their homes, workplaces and neighbourhoods as He empowered their witness to the resurrected Jesus (see John 7:39; Acts 1:4–8).

But who or what is this Spirit?

Many people have questions about the Holy Spirit. Is the Spirit a person? Is the Spirit divine—co-equal with Jesus and the Father? How did Jesus relate to the Spirit? What does it mean to be baptised by the Spirit? What is the relationship between the baptism of the Spirit and empowerment for life and witness? How does the metaphor of rain relate to the mission of the church? What must I do to experience a daily filling of the Spirit, and what can I expect to happen if I am filled? What difference will it make to my relationship with God and others? What will it look like? What will my family, friends and colleagues see? This book explores these questions and many more.

Unfortunately, the Spirit is neglected by many—often resisted and rejected. Some fear being caught up in excessive behaviour, or even being tricked or trapped by evil spirits. We will examine some of these concerns.

It is my prayer that as you read this book you will be refreshed by the Spirit's thirst-quenching presence, bask in His fellowship, witness His love for you, your family and community, and be empowered for sharing by His baptism.

Getting started

At the end of each chapter in this book, there are questions with key Bible verses to read that will point you to an empowered life. You could start a social media group with friends to explore your discoveries or plan a regular small group catch-up for discussion and application. Having read the key scriptures and the chapter from this book—and after reflecting on your relationship with the Spirit—you might also use the *Discovery Bible Reading* questions as a frame for discussion (see Appendix A):

1. What was new?
2. What surprised us?
3. What do we not understand?
4. What would we obey or apply to our lives?
5. What will we share with another person this week—and with whom?

If you are thirsty, you can be Spirit-filled.

EMPOWERED

1. How do you feel about your current relationship with the Spirit?

2. What are your hopes and expectations for revitalisation and empowerment?

CHAPTER 1

IF YOU ARE THIRSTY

> On the last day, the climax of the festival [of Shelters], Jesus stood and shouted to the crowds, "*Anyone who is thirsty* may come to me! Anyone who believes in me may come and drink! For the Scriptures declare, 'Rivers of living water will flow from his heart.' (When he said "living water," he was speaking of the Spirit, who would be given to everyone believing in him. But the Spirit had not yet been given, because Jesus had not yet entered into his glory) (John 7:37–39, emphasis added).

It was a sensational announcement, His most important. The crowds knew it, as did the temple authorities, priests and Pharisees, leaving them bitterly divided.

Some were sure He was "the Prophet"—the one expected before the promised Messiah's arrival. Others were just as certain that He was the Messiah, but still others were doubtful. "He can't be!" they concluded. "'Will the Messiah come from Galilee?'...So the crowd was divided about him" (John 7:40–43).

Some wanted Him arrested. Temple guards were sent by priests and Pharisees to bring Him in. They returned empty-handed, reporting, "We have never heard anyone speak like this!" (John 7:46).

Setting the stage

Before going to Jerusalem, Jesus had been in Galilee, well out of reach of the Jewish leaders who were plotting to kill Him (see John 7:1). His own brothers ridiculed Him: "Leave here and go to Judea, where your followers can see your miracles! You can't become famous if you hide like this! If you can do such wonderful things, show yourself to the world!" (John 7:4, 5). Jesus would go to Jerusalem—but it wasn't to increase His popularity by performing miracles. He had other plans, in accordance with His Father's agenda.

His brothers left for Jerusalem and, a short time later, Jesus also set out on the week-long journey, travelling "secretly, staying out of public view" (John 7:10). In Jerusalem, the Jewish leaders were determined to track Him down and "there was a lot of grumbling about him among the crowds." Some considered Him "a good man," but others said, "He's nothing but a fraud" (see John 7:11–13). Quietly and unobtrusively moving among them, Jesus no doubt heard it all.

"Then, midway through the festival" (John 7:14), the scene changed. Jesus stepped out. The apostle John simply records, "Jesus went up to the Temple and began to teach" (John 7:14). Why the dramatic shift? Why at this time? He could not have chosen a more public forum and He was obviously ready for confrontation. What was He doing? Where was this leading?

Water-drawing and water-pouring

During the final days of the Sukkot festival, with Jesus speaking publicly and the Jewish authorities seemingly unable or unwilling to stop Him, the question on the lips of many of the locals was, "Could our leaders possibly believe that he is the Messiah?" (John 7:26).

Jesus fuelled the tensions over His identity. When teaching in the temple area, He called out in the hearing of the priests and people, "Yes, you know me, and you know where I come from. But I'm not here on my own. The one who sent me is true, and you don't know him. But I know him because I come from him, and he sent me to you" (John 7:28, 29).

Early each morning during Sukkot, as a reminder of past deliverance and as a promise of refreshment to come, priests descended the steep steps to the pool of Siloam to draw water, then carried it up to the temple altar.[1] In the 8th century BC, in the days of King Hezekiah, the Assyrian armies attacked Israel to the north and threatened Jerusalem. To safe-guard the city in preparation for the siege, a 533-metre-long tunnel (about a third of a mile) was dug to bring water from the Gihon Spring in the Kedron Valley into this pool within the city walls (see 2 Kings 20:20).

Following the destruction of Jerusalem by the Babylonians in the 6th century BC, Nehemiah returned to rebuild the city. At that time, "the wall of the pool of Siloam near the king's garden" (Nehemiah 3:15) was also repaired. As the city's only well, the pool of Siloam held profound messianic meaning, reminding the nation of their dependence on God as their well of salvation.

Now, holding high a golden vessel with Kedron water from the pool of Siloam, the priests led the worshipping multitudes up the steep Herodian Street steps to the altar of sacrifice. There, with the pilgrims singing the Hallel psalms (Psalms 113–118) and dancing in joyful celebration, the vessel of water from the well of salvation together with temple wine were poured as an offering into basins on the altar. Through conduits and pipes, the water and wine then flowed from the altar back into the Kedron Valley and toward the Dead Sea.

Every aspect of the ceremony—the water-drawing at the pool, the water-pouring at the altar of sacrifice, and the water flowing down the deep ravines of the Kedron Valley through the Judean wilderness to the Dead Sea—had deep prophetic, messianic and emotional significance to the people.

A river of life

Had not the prophet Ezekiel written of their deliverance, using this very setting with his vision of the river of healing? He saw "a stream flowing east from beneath the door of the temple and passing to the right of the altar." And out to the eastern side of the temple walls, he saw "the water flowing out through the south side of the east gateway." Each time he was told to cross the Kedron valley, the water was deeper, until "the river was too deep to cross without swimming" (see Ezekiel 47:1–5).

Then, to his amazement, Ezekiel saw trees growing on the banks and was told:

> This river flows east through the desert into the valley of the Dead Sea. The waters of this stream will make the salty waters of the Dead Sea fresh and pure. There will be swarms of living things wherever the water of this river flows (Ezekiel 47:8, 9).

He saw the Dead Sea teeming with fish, and fishermen with their nets along the shores. "Fruit trees of all kinds" (Ezekiel 47:12) flourished on the riverbanks, in what had been the most forbidding desert wilderness, and he was told:

> There will always be fruit on their branches. There will be a new crop every month, for they are watered by the river flowing from the Temple. The fruit will be for food and the leaves for healing (Ezekiel 47:12).[2]

Pointing to the refreshing that the Messiah would bring, this vision was the hope of Israel.

For the pilgrims in the temple courts, the water-pouring ceremony at the altar of sacrifice also reminded them of Moses striking the rock for water in the desert (see Exodus 17:6; Numbers 20:8–11; 1 Corinthians 10:1–4). This rock also represented Christ—the One who would give life.

The festival of Sukkot took place at the end of the hot, dry summer months, after the last crops had been gathered. With the countryside parched, thirsting for the early rains expected at any time, refreshing rain and water from "the wells of salvation" (Isaiah 12:3, NIV) were a central feature of this festival. It was a ceremony of rich prophetic significance, pointing to the hope of all Israel, the coming of the Messiah and His Spirit, to bring life, refreshment and healing.

Camped out in rough shelters made of branches and exposed to the elements, reminiscent of their wilderness years, the pilgrims recounted stories of God's protection and their deliverance from Egyptian slavery. They bemoaned their current fate, enslaved under Rome and burdened by corrupt religious authorities. They were thirsty for freedom, autonomy and salvation.

And now, on the last and greatest day of the feast, the attention of the crowd was on the priests holding high the golden vessels of water and wine to pour them out at the altar of sacrifice. It was a moment of high drama. Trumpets blew and hearts rejoiced.

Then, in the midst of the ceremony, Jesus stood up. At His baptism, John the Baptist had announced, "He is the one who baptises with the Holy Spirit" (John 1:33)—and now, He shouted to the crowds:

> "Anyone who is thirsty may come to me! Anyone who believes in me may come and drink! For the Scriptures declare, 'Rivers of living water will flow from his heart'" (John 7:37, 38).

Jesus is the well of salvation

Standing close to the altar, Jesus' invitation—"Anyone who is thirsty may come to me!"—was His most significant announcement. His meaning was unmistakable. Jesus was announcing, *I am the well of your salvation, your source of life. I am the Anointed One, the Messiah.* He was declaring, *I am the source of living water.*

He was the One foreshadowed by the water-pouring ceremony. He was the One spoken of in the prophecies recited that day—the Lord of salvation and Giver of the Holy Spirit (see Jeremiah 17:13; Ezekiel 36:24–27).

Jesus' invitation—"Anyone who is thirsty may come to me!"—was His most significant announcement.

What He had shared privately with His apostles at Caesarea Philippi a few weeks before (see Matthew 16:21), He now announced for all to hear. The reaction was immediate. The crowd was stunned. "When the crowds heard him say this, some of them declared, 'Surely this man is the Prophet we've been expecting.' Others said, 'He is the Messiah'" (John 7:40, 41).

The Holy Spirit is the living water

Quoting the prophets, Jesus promised that "rivers of living water" would flow from the hearts of those who believed Him (see John 7:38). The water and wine poured out at the altar formed but a trickle into the Kedron and eventually was just a drop in the Dead Sea. The literal water poured out did little to refresh the land. But Jesus reinterpreted the prophecies, declaring that from the hearts of believing disciples rivers of living water would flow to refresh others—their families, friends, colleagues and communities. In this book, these are referred to as a person's *relational streams*.

The apostle John explained that when speaking of living water, Jesus "was speaking of the Spirit, who would be given to everyone believing in him." Then, to clarify further, John wrote, "But the Spirit had not yet been given, because Jesus had not yet entered into his glory" (John 7:39).

When speaking of living water, Jesus "was speaking of the Spirit."

Why did John write that "the Spirit had not yet been given"? Who is this Spirit, and why is He like living water? We will explore the person and role of the Holy Spirit in the next chapter.

EMPOWERED

Read John 7:1–9:41.

1. Imagine listening to the reactions on the Temple Mount, or visiting families gathered in booths around the city that evening. What is your experience as you hear:
   - The agitated, angry arguments among priests and Pharisees?

   - The buzz of discussion and excitement of pilgrims? Jesus' outburst confirmed to some that He was crazy. Who else would shout loud enough to stop the thousands of singing, praying and dancing pilgrims in the temple courts? But might He be the Messiah?

- What do you hear as you listen in on the embarrassment or disbelief of His brothers? They had made it clear that they had no confidence in Him, but what now?

2. Reflect on how Jesus gave new meaning to Ezekiel's prophecy of the river of healing (see Ezekiel 47:1–12) and the water-drawing and water-pouring celebrations of the Feast of Shelters (see John 7:37–39):

Prophetic symbols	**Fulfilment of prophecy for all people**
Siloam, the city's well	Jesus, the well of salvation
Water from the well	The living water of the Holy Spirit
Pouring out the water	Jesus poured out in sacrifice
Water flowing into the Kedron and out through the wilderness	The Spirit flowing from believers into the lives of others
Healing of Israel's deserts and the Dead Sea	All people hearing the words of life through the witness of believers

What further implications do you see in how Jesus reinterpreted Ezekiel's prophecy?

3. What are you thirsty for? What is the deepest desire of your heart? How do you feel about the Holy Spirit being living water—for you, in your circumstances?

CHAPTER 2

LIVING WATER

> Jesus replied, "If you only knew the gift God has for you and who you are speaking to, you would ask me, and I would give you living water" (John 4:10).

Jesus called the Spirit *living water* (see John 7:38, 39). But who is this Spirit, and what does the name Spirit mean? Is the Spirit a person? Is the Spirit divine—co-equal with Jesus and the Father? How did Jesus relate to the Spirit? And what does this mean to us and our relationship with God?

Jesus' life and ministry were intertwined with the Spirit. To the desperately broken Samaritan woman, Jesus offered the Spirit, the living water, promising that "those who drink the water I give will never be thirsty again." He added, "It becomes a fresh, bubbling spring within them, giving them eternal life" (John 4:14).

Of Jesus, it was prophesied:

> And the Spirit of the Lord will rest on him—the Spirit of wisdom and understanding, the Spirit of counsel and might, the Spirit of knowledge and the fear of the Lord. He will delight in obeying the Lord, He will not judge by appearance, nor make a decision based on hearsay. He will give justice to the poor and make fair decisions for the exploited.... He will wear righteousness like a belt and truth like an undergarment (Isaiah 11:2–5).

He knew the Spirit. He was conceived, anointed and filled by the Spirit, and He taught and ministered through the Spirit's presence and power. This inter-relationship, together with the Father, was described by the 4th-century Cappadocian fathers (in modern-day Turkey, Cappadocia, was an early centre of Christian activity) as *perichoresis*—suggesting an inclusive, intimate, divine dance.[1]

In downtown Dubai, on the 12-hectare Burj Khalifa Lake, you can see delightfully choreographed dancing fountains, where the music, colour and movement of the water makes a singular, spectacular scene. It is a beautiful sight to behold. In a similar way, the Father, Jesus and the Spirit are as one, working in beautiful harmony.

Is the Spirit a Person—and how can we know?

While much of Christianity has been defined by statements of faith, we cannot know God simply by giving intellectual assent to some statements as true. Jesus grounded faith and scriptural truth in the application, saying, "You are truly my disciples if you *remain faithful* to my teachings [or *hold* to my teachings, NIV]. And you will know the truth, and the truth will set you free" (John 8:31, 32).

Jesus' first followers came to understand God through concrete practices—baptism, the laying on of hands, the Lord's Supper, prayer, anointing with oil, miracles, worship, witness, and conversations about their Lord's resurrection and His Spirit's presence. These foster faith, hope and love, and through them we experience God's living presence in our lives.

In his journey of faith, Paul experienced the Holy Spirit as a person with a mind (see Romans 8:27), knowledge and determination (see 1 Corinthians 2:11, 12:11; Acts 15:28). He describes the Spirit as loving (see Romans 15:30), as a person who enjoys fellowship and conversation (see 2 Corinthians 13:14), and who can be insulted and grieved (see Hebrews 10:29; Ephesians 4:30).

The Spirit calls people to follow Jesus (see Revelation 22:17), living within and testifying that we are "God's children" (see Romans 8:11, 16). He instructs (see 1 Timothy 4:1), helps and intercedes (see Romans 8:26, 27), and distributes spiritual gifts (see 1 Corinthians 12:1, 11).

While there is much we do not understand—and while the Spirit is more than the *persons* we see around us, and One to whom we cannot ascribe gender—we usually speak of the Godhead, including the Spirit, with male prepositions.

What does His name mean?

Most of us know the meaning of our names. In the Hebrew, the name "Spirit" is *ruach* and its Greek equivalent is *pneuma*. The basic meaning of these words is "wind" or "breath." However, the name "Spirit" also reflects the creativity or power within the wind that sets other things into motion—just as the waves that relentlessly break on the shore are caused by the movement of air across the ocean.[2]

The name "Spirit" reflects the creativity or power within the wind that sets other things into motion.

His name takes on added meaning and power when associated with other divine names, as with *Ruach Elohim* (Spirit of God, Genesis 1:2), *Ruach YHWH* (Spirit of Yahweh or Spirit of the LORD, Isaiah 59:19), *Ruach Hakman* (Spirit of Wisdom, Isaiah 11:2), and *Ruach Hakkodesh* (Holy Spirit, Psalm 51:11; Isaiah 63:10, 11, 14). This added meaning is also reflected when He is identified as the invisible but powerful Holy *pneuma* in the New Testament.

How did Jesus relate to Him? And what does that mean for us?

The evening before His betrayal, Jesus was intent on helping His disciples understand the unique relationship they would have with the Holy Spirit after His death and resurrection. Although they struggled to understand what He was saying, Jesus' words have much to tell us about the relationship between the Spirit and Himself, and also about the role of the Holy Spirit in our lives.

Jesus had been the disciples' counsellor and guide for more than three years, but He was about to leave. Jesus wanted them to know that they would have "another Advocate" (John 14:16, 26)—also called the "Spirit of truth" (John 14:17), "the Spirit of Christ" or "Spirit of God" (Romans 8:9). Jesus went on to explain how close the Holy Spirit was to Himself and to the Father: "the Advocate, the Holy Spirit, *whom the Father will send in my name*, will teach you all things and remind you of everything *I have said to you*" (John 14:26, NIV). Further, "When the Advocate comes, *whom I will send to you from the Father*—the Spirit of truth who goes out from the Father—*he will testify about me*" (John 15:26, NIV).

Jesus indicated an intimate bond between the Father, Himself and the Spirit. "All that belongs to the Father is mine," He said. "That is why I said the Spirit will receive from me what he will make known to you" (John 16:15, NIV). The Spirit speaks and acts in harmony with Jesus and the Father. In a sense, the presence of the Spirit is also the presence of Jesus and the Father (see John 16:16; compare John 14:18–23).

Jesus indicated an intimate bond between the Father, Himself and the Spirit . . . The Spirit speaks and acts in harmony with Jesus and the Father.

So what did that mean for the disciples—and for us? Jesus outlined several ways in which the Holy Spirit would work in our lives. "The world cannot accept him, because it neither sees him nor knows him. But," Jesus affirmed, "you know him, for *he lives with you and will be in you*" (John 14:17, NIV). He also told the disciples that the

Holy Spirit would remind them of His words (see John 14:26), testify of Him (see John 15:26), and teach them about sin, righteousness and judgment (see John 16:8). Jesus had "much more to say"—more than they could bear. "But," He said, "when he, the Spirit of truth, comes, *he will guide you into all the truth.* He will not speak on his own; he will speak only what he hears, and *he will tell you what is yet to come. He will glorify me* because it is from me that he will receive what he will make known to you" (John 16:12–14, NIV).

Clearly, to Jesus, the Holy Spirit is vitally important for our Christian experience and mission. Jesus speaks of the Holy Spirit as His colleague, associate, representative and equal—our counsellor, teacher and guide. This draws us to reflect on the relationship between the Father, the Spirit and Jesus, and whether the Spirit is a divine being equal with them.

Is the Spirit an equal person in the triune Godhead?

The Spirit is described as "the eternal Spirit"[3] (Hebrews 9:14), "the power of the Most High" (Luke 1:35), everywhere present (see Psalm 139:7–10), and one who knows the "deep things" and "thoughts of God" (1 Corinthians 2:10, 11, NIV). These are four distinct divine qualities of Father, Son and Spirit—eternal, omnipotent, omnipresent and omniscient.

The Spirit does the works of God—creating (see Job 33:4; Psalm 104:30), giving life (see John 6:63; Romans 8:11) and inspiring (see 2 Samuel 23:2; 2 Peter 1:21; compare 2 Timothy 3:16). He is called the Spirit of truth (see John 14:17, NIV), the life-giving Spirit (see Romans 8:2), the Spirit of wisdom and revelation (see Ephesians 1:17, NIV), the Spirit of grace (see Hebrews 10:29, NIV) and of glory (see 1 Peter 4:14, NIV).

What is more, He bears the names of God, including Jehovah. This name is a translator's designation for the divine name YHWH, referred to as the *tetragrammaton* and usually capitalised as "LORD" in English Bibles.[4] The words of "the LORD Almighty" in Isaiah 6:1–10 are attributed to the Holy Spirit in Acts 28:25–27—equating the Spirit with Jehovah.

When Ananias and Sapphira conspired to give the appearance of generously donating the full proceeds of the sale of their property to help out suffering believers, while secretly keeping some for themselves, the apostle Peter called them out. They had "lied to the Holy Spirit" (Acts 5:3) and in doing this, he stressed, "You have not lied to men *but to God*" (Acts 5:4).

The Spirit is God—a divine being. He is one in power and glory with the Father and the Son. He has all the attributes of God, but at the same time is a distinct, divine person.

Equal, yet distinct!

They belong together, yet the Father, Son and Spirit are each distinct, divine persons. This was evident during Jesus' lifetime.

At His baptism, the Spirit descended on Jesus while the Father's voice was heard from heaven speaking in commendation of His Son (see Matthew 3:16, 17; Luke 3:21, 22).[5] The inauguration of Jesus' ministry on the banks of the Jordan brought the three persons of the Godhead "strikingly to view."[6] An early Christian saying was, "Go to Jordan and thou shalt see the Trinity."[7]

In His promise of the Spirit's ministry, which would follow His own, Jesus made a clear distinction between Himself, His Father and the Spirit, saying: "I [Jesus] will ask the Father, and he [the Father] will give you another Advocate [Holy Spirit]" (John 14:16).

And in His commission for His followers to multiply disciples, Jesus linked the names of Father, Son and Holy Spirit in an extraordinarily significant manner. He commanded them to: "Go and make disciples of all the nations, baptising them in the name of the Father and the Son and the Holy Spirit" (Matthew 28:19).

As Christians, we believe that there is one God, who is the Father, the Son and the Holy Spirit. Or, to put it another way, the Father who is unseen is revealed in the Son and made present in the lives of believers by the Spirit.

The Spirit bears the attributes, names and character of God. He is a distinct person of the Godhead,[8] but He cannot be limited by our ideas of personhood. God makes His "home" with us (see John 14:23, NIV) and does every special work in our lives through the Holy Spirit—the living water.

EMPOWERED

Read John 13:1–16:33.

1. The evening before His betrayal and death, Jesus talked with His disciples about the Holy Spirit. How did you feel reading what He shared with them?

2. What have been your most valued discoveries from Jesus' words that evening?

3. Jesus' repeated references to the Spirit point to His essential, vital work and role in our lives. What have you decided to prioritise?

CHAPTER 3

IT'S THE SPIRIT'S ERA

It is now the Spirit's time.

Some think the true *zeitgeist* of an era—the social and political mood, literally "the spirit of the times"—cannot be known until it is over. This might be true, but we hardly need to wait to see that COVID-19, globalisation, urbanisation, global warming, environmental concerns, migration, glocalisation, the pervasive power of the internet and changing values are clearly defining the spirit and spirituality of the first decades of this century.

But they are not the only factors defining our times. We live in the age of the Holy Spirit. His time continues—it is His epoch, His era. Jesus foretold it.

As we saw in Chapter 1, on the last and greatest day of the Feast of Shelters, Jesus promised living water for thirsty pilgrims. In parenthesis, the apostle John made it clear that Jesus "was speaking of the Spirit, who would be given to everyone believing in him. But," John wrote, "the Spirit had not yet been given, because Jesus had not yet entered into his glory" (John 7:39)—or "been glorified" (NIV).

What did John mean? What was holding the Spirit back?

A new era

The Spirit features in the first Bible story and is mentioned more than 90 times in 22 of the Old Testament books. He is also central to the first New Testament account, overshadowing Mary who gave birth to Jesus "the holy one . . . the Son of God" (Luke 1:35, NIV). And from then, He was fully active in and through Jesus—anointing, leading, filling and empowering. So how could it be said that "the Spirit had not yet been given" (John 7:39)?

Clearly Jesus and John were pointing to a new era. John pointed out that the time of the Spirit would begin when Jesus was glorified. This points to two historic realities that are foundational to Christian faith—Calvary and Pentecost. And these events are inextricably linked.

In Jesus, God came into our world in human form. That is why He was also named Immanuel, meaning "God is with us" (Matthew 1:23). He was born in humble circumstances, in Bethlehem in the days of Herod the Great, and welcomed by shepherds and foreign magi. He grew and became a builder, working with wood and stone. Then after three and a half years of public ministry demonstrating the principles of the kingdom of Heaven, Jesus rode into Jerusalem on Palm Sunday and predicted His hideous death, saying, "the time has come for the Son of Man to enter into his glory" (John 12:23). He prayed, "Father, bring glory to your name" (John 12:28). Immediately, a voice like thunder "spoke from heaven, saying, 'I have already brought glory to my name, and I will do so again'" (John 12:28). Jesus explained, "The time for judging this world has come. . . . And when I am lifted up from the earth, I will draw everyone to myself" (John 12:31, 32).

Days later, Jesus was crucified as the Passover Lamb. At Calvary outside Jerusalem, He was derided by Roman and Jewish authorities as a traitor and criminal. He was covered with blood and spit, beaten and bruised, naked for all to shame and mock—and the glory of God was seen. The heart of God was revealed, as His justice and mercy for sinners kissed. At

Calvary, Jesus was *glorified*. And this glory has been drawing people ever since.

Three days later, Jesus rose from the grave—victorious over sin, the evil one and death. Forty days after that, He rose to heaven and was welcomed to God's right hand. At Calvary, He was seen in the glory of His grace and at Pentecost, He entered His Father's glorious presence. In this way the stage was set for the Spirit's greatest work. Having accomplished everything necessary for our salvation, Jesus left—and then it was the Spirit's time.

At Calvary, Jesus was covered with blood and spit, beaten and bruised, naked for all to shame and mock—and the glory of God was seen. . . . At Calvary, Jesus was glorified.

Jesus explained the transition:

> And I will ask the Father, and he will give you another Advocate, who will never leave you. He is the Holy Spirit, who leads into all truth. The world cannot receive him, because it isn't looking for him and doesn't recognise him. But you know him, because he lives with you now and later will be in you (John 14:16, 17).

Note Jesus' emphasis on the future—the time after Calvary when at Pentecost the Father would give the Spirit. On the day of Pentecost—50 days after His resurrection—Jesus *entered His glory*. He had been received back to heaven 10 days earlier, but now, in answer to the disciples' earnest prayers, something special happened:

> On the day of Pentecost all the believers were meeting together in one place. Suddenly, there was a sound from heaven like the roaring of a mighty windstorm, and it

> filled the house where they were sitting. Then, what looked like flames or tongues of fire appeared and settled on each of them. And everyone present was filled with the Holy Spirit and began speaking in other languages, as the Holy Spirit gave them this ability (Acts 2:1–4).

To the crowds in the streets of Jerusalem, Peter explained what had happened in heaven:

> God raised Jesus from the dead, and we are all witnesses of this. Now he is exalted to the place of highest honour in heaven, at God's right hand. And the Father, as he had promised, gave him the Holy Spirit to pour out upon us, just as you see and hear today (Acts 2:32, 33).

It was the beginning of a new era.

It was the Spirit's time!

The Spirit's special time comes after Calvary and Pentecost. Jesus, whose ministry in human form was limited by time and space, was replaced on earth by the Spirit "who will *never* leave you" and who "will be in you" (John 14:16, 17). Key transition ideas are illustrated in the following diagram.

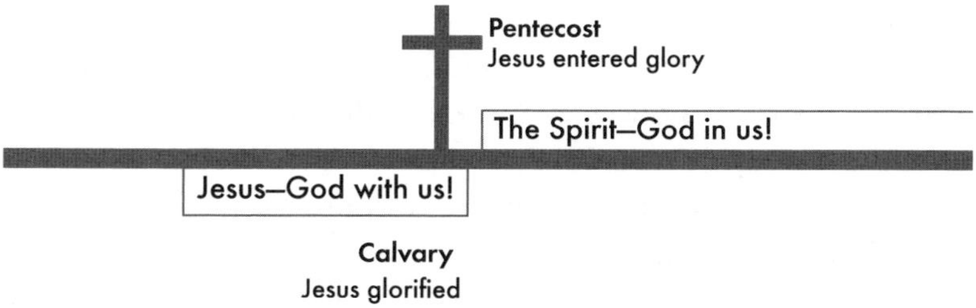

The transition from Jesus' life with us to the Spirit's presence in us.

When Jesus told His followers about the coming of the Spirit, they struggled to understand what He was saying. He was telling them that He was leaving—and surely that was a bad thing. But He reassured them, saying, "It is actually best for you that I go away, because if I don't, the Advocate won't come" (John 16:7). He promised:

> I will not abandon you as orphans—I will come to you. Soon the world will no longer see me, but you will see me.... When I am raised to life again, you will know that I am in my Father, and you are in me, and I am in you (John 14:18–20).

It is through the presence of the Spirit that Jesus' guarantee to all who love Him is realised. He declared, "My Father will love them, and we will come and make our home with each of them" (John 14:23). What amazing love and grace! Through Jesus' salvation and the Spirit's indwelling presence, the Almighty Triune God delights to make His home in us—in you and me.

The day of Pentecost marked the beginning of this new era of the Spirit.

The day of Pentecost marked the beginning of this new era of the Spirit. Jesus' life, death, resurrection and ascension were preparatory and foundational—radically changing everything. The task of His followers was being redefined. They were now in "the last days" (Acts 2:17; compare Hebrews 1:1, 2). Jesus' ongoing role would be different, as would be that of the Spirit. Once Jesus had done His work, the Spirit could do His greatest work. But, without the Spirit's coming, all Jesus did would have little impact.

His coming at Pentecost was called a baptism.

EMPOWERED

Re-read John 14:5–31.

1. What was then holding the Spirit back, and what might now restrain Him?

2. Why do you think Jesus' death and resurrection were preparatory to the Spirit doing His greatest work for us? What have you discovered to be His work for you?

3. On the Thursday night, around the meal in the upper room, Jesus told His disciples, "When I am raised to life again, you will know that I am in my Father, and you are in me, and I am in you" (John 14:20). What does this mean to you, and how do you feel about it?

4. In what ways has the Spirit set up "home" for the Father, Jesus and Himself with you (John 14:23)? What does this mean for you and your family?

CHAPTER 4

WHAT IS HOLY SPIRIT BAPTISM?

Between Calvary and Pentecost, Jesus told His followers, "In a few days you will be baptised with [or in] the Holy Spirit" (Acts 1:5).[1]

What does being baptised with the Spirit look like? What will our families, friends and colleagues see? Is Spirit baptism essential or is it optional? Is it integral to conversion or a later experience? What difference does it really make? How can we be baptised and filled with the Spirit and know it?

How can we be baptised and filled with the Spirit and know it?

The emphasis on speaking in tongues, sometimes with crying, shouting and falling down, concerns many, even frightening some away from engaging with the Holy Spirit. Once considered fanatical, unbalanced extremes, are these manifestations now to be accepted as normal behaviour for those baptised with the Spirit?

Spirit baptism is from Jesus

Standing at a muddy stream in the desert at the lowest spot on earth—only five kilometres (three miles) north of the Dead Sea, and a short distance from Jericho to the west and Mount Nebo to the east—John the Baptist cut a strange, rough figure. He lived in the stifling heat of the Jordan rift valley. He wore garments of camel hair with a leather belt, living on grasshoppers and wild honey.[2] He looked, sounded and probably smelt like an Old Testament prophet.[3] The crowds flocked to him. Mark records, "The whole Judean countryside and all the people of Jerusalem went out to him" (Mark 1:5, NIV).

His conception was a miracle, and he was "filled with the Holy Spirit, even before his birth" (Luke 1:15). Now John was baptising people at the Jordan river, a place filled with significance for the Jewish people. It was this river that the Israelites had crossed centuries before to enter the Promised Land. It was where Elisha had pled for a double portion of the spirit of Elijah. And it was near where Naaman the Syrian leper begrudgingly dipped in the dirty waters, obeying Elisha's instructions for cleansing. It is little wonder the crowds were asking, "Who are you?" (John 1:21).

Was he Elijah returned? Or Moses? Was he the Messiah they longed for? Would he be a courageous revolutionary like Judas Maccabeus, who saved them from Hellenisation and idolatry almost two centuries before? Would he deliver them from their Roman oppressors?

John the Baptist's response was clear: he was not the Messiah nor Elijah. Rather, in the words of the prophet Isaiah, he declared, "I am the voice of one calling in the wilderness, 'Make straight the way for the Lord'" (John 1:23, NIV). When asked about his authority to baptise, John declared:

> "I baptise you with water for repentance. But after me comes one who is more powerful than I, whose sandals I am not worthy to carry. He will baptise you with the Holy Spirit and with fire" (Matthew 3:11, NIV).

His prophecy that Jesus "will baptise you with [in] the Holy Spirit" was recorded by all four gospel writers—with Matthew and Luke adding the phrase, "and with fire" (see Matthew 3:11; Mark 1:8; Luke 3:16; John 1:32, 33). The apostle John tied John the Baptist's prophecy to Jesus' anointing by the Spirit, explaining, "the one who sent me to baptise with water told me, 'The man on whom you see the Spirit come down and remain is the one who will baptise with [in] the Holy Spirit'" (John 1:33, NIV).

John the Baptist pointed to the distinctively timeless ministry of Jesus:

> He "*takes away* the sin of the world" (John 1:29).
>
> He "*baptises in* the Holy Spirit" (John 1:33, NASB).

Jesus continues to do these two things. John was called "the Baptist" because he baptised in waters of repentance, but Jesus is the baptiser who continues to take away sin and baptise in the Holy Spirit.[4] These were the two promised blessings of the new covenant predicted by Old Testament prophets.[5] Isaiah, Jeremiah, Ezekiel and Joel promised "a liberal" outpouring of the Spirit "which would be new and distinctive."[6] John the Baptist, "the last prophet of the old order, summarised this expectation"[7] when he declared, "[Jesus] will baptise with the Holy Spirit" (John 1:33).

Jesus is the baptiser who continues to take away sin and baptise in the Holy Spirit… the two promised blessings of the new covenant.

Spirit baptism is an exclusively New Testament expression, referred to seven times in three types of references: there are (i) prophecies, (ii) verses that tell of these prophecies being fulfilled, and (iii) scriptures that teach about this experience.

Promises of Spirit baptism

Of the five prophetic references promising a future experience of Spirit baptism, four were from the beginning of Jesus' ministry—John the Baptist's prophecy that Jesus would baptise with the Spirit (see Matthew 3:11; Mark 1:8; Luke 3:16; John 1:32, 33). During His ministry, especially in His last months and days, Jesus focused on the Spirit's promised coming (see John 7:37–39, 14:16–16:15). The fifth prophetic reference to Spirit baptism was made by Jesus after Calvary and His resurrection, just before His ascension to the glory of His Father's throne. He commanded His followers:

> Do not leave Jerusalem until the Father sends you the gift he promised, as I told you before. John baptised with water, but in just a few days you will be baptised with [in] the Holy Spirit (Acts 1:4, 5).

In addition to the promises above, on resurrection Sunday evening, Jesus "breathed" on His startled disciples, saying, "Receive the Holy Spirit" (John 20:22). This was also a promise of Spirit baptism, which would only be fully realised on Pentecost, after He returned to the Father.

The Holy Spirit was active in Old Testament times, but there was no baptism of the Spirit prior to Calvary. He could not do His greatest work until everything necessary for our salvation was completed.

Fulfilment of the promises

Forty days after His resurrection, Jesus ascended to heaven while His disciples waited in Jerusalem, where they met continually for prayer (see Acts 1:14). Ten days later:

> On the day of Pentecost, all the believers were meeting together in one place. Suddenly, there was a sound

> from heaven like the roaring of a mighty windstorm, and it filled the house where they were sitting. Then, what looked like flames or tongues of fire appeared and settled on each of them. And everyone present was filled with the Holy Spirit and began speaking in other languages, as the Holy Spirit gave them this ability (Acts 2:1–4).

Crowded in the narrow streets below, pilgrims asked each other, "What can this mean?" Peter shouted to the crowd, "What you see was predicted long ago by the prophet Joel: 'In the last days,' God said, 'I will pour out my Spirit upon all people'" (Acts 2:16, 17). He then explained:

> God publicly endorsed Jesus of Nazareth by doing powerful miracles, wonders, and signs through him, as you well know. But . . . with the help of lawless Gentiles, you nailed him to a cross and killed him. But God released him from the horrors of death and raised him back to life.
>
> God raised Jesus from the dead, and we all are witnesses of this. Now he is exalted to the place of highest honour in heaven, at God's right hand. And the Father, as he had promised, gave him the Holy Spirit to pour out upon us, just as you see and hear today (Acts 2:22–24, 32, 33).

Deeply convicted of their guilt in crucifying their "Lord and Messiah," the crowds cried out, "Brothers, what should we do?" Peter responded, "Each of you must repent of your sins and turn to God, and be baptised in the name of Jesus Christ *for the forgiveness of your sins. Then you will receive the gift of the Holy Spirit*" (Acts 2:36–38).

On Pentecost day, "those who believed what Peter said were baptised and added to the church...about 3000 in all" (Acts 2:41). It was not a mass baptism—the nearest river and sea were two days' walk away, and the people were baptised "that day". They may have been baptised in Jewish ritual cleansing pools in homes and at the southern steps of the temple. By water and Spirit baptism, they became part of the body of Christ.

Spirit baptism is not optional

It is essential. The apostle Peter pointed to the two blessings John the Baptist had promised—Jesus will *take away sin* and also *baptise in the Holy Spirit*—adding, "This promise is to you, to your children, and to those far away—all who have been called by the Lord our God." He urged his listeners strongly, 'Save yourselves from this crooked generation!'" (Acts 2:39, 40).

Nothing could be clearer: Spirit baptism is essential for all followers of Jesus.

As illustrated below, the promises and prophecies of Holy Spirit baptism reached their fulfilment on Pentecost day: the 120 as well as the 3000 "were filled with the Holy Spirit" (Acts 2:4); and "the promised Holy Spirit" was "received from the Father" and "poured out" upon them by Jesus (Acts 2:33, NIV).

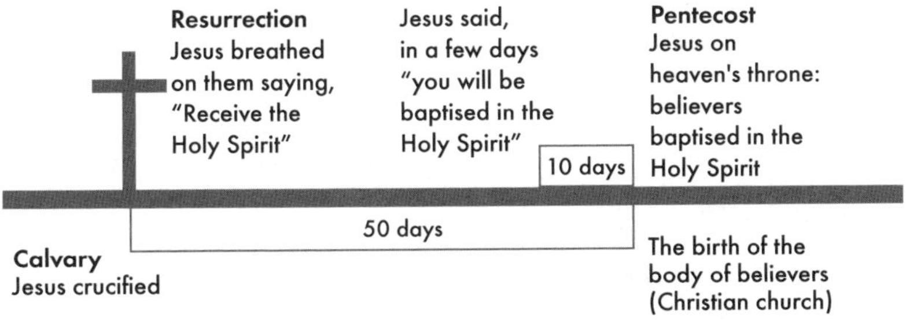

The prophecies of Holy Spirit baptism were fulfilled on Pentecost day.

The prophecies of Spirit baptism—and the fulfilment stories—show that the outpouring on the day of Pentecost marked both the beginning of the Spirit's era and the birth of the Christian church.

The evidence of Spirit baptism

The promises and fulfilment scriptures, along with Peter's explanation and appeals on Pentecost day, provide important insights into Spirit baptism. In addition to these, the Bible also contains teaching scriptures explaining the meaning and impact of being baptised by the Spirit, and how to know whether you have received this baptism.

Acts 1:8 is the clearest teaching scripture on the purpose of Spirit baptism. Just before His ascension, Jesus told His disciples:

> But you will receive power when the Holy Spirit comes upon you. And you will be my witnesses, telling people about me everywhere—in Jerusalem, throughout Judea, in Samaria, and to the ends of the earth (Acts 1:8).

And this is exactly what happened. When the Spirit fell on the waiting disciples on the day of Pentecost, they declared "the wonderful things God [had] done" in the languages of the people gathering on the street below (see Acts 2:1–4, 11). Many godly Jewish pilgrims, visiting Jerusalem from across the Roman empire and beyond, came running. Crowding the narrow streets, they heard Galileans speaking in their mother languages and dialects.[8] As Kenneth Kuas, coordinator of Volunteers in Action in Madang and Manus Provinces, Papua New Guinea, so aptly put it, "The Spirit empowered the believers to share the gospel in the heart languages of the people."[9]

In the longer ending of Mark, Jesus is reported saying that the gospel will be shared in "new languages," indicating languages *known* to those hearing but *new* to those witnessing (Mark

16:17).[10] And this is what happened. Luke makes this point three times:

- "They were bewildered *to hear their own languages being spoken* by the believers" (Acts 2:6).
- "They were completely amazed. 'How can this be?' they exclaimed. 'These people are all from Galilee, and yet we hear them speaking *in our own native languages*!'" (Acts 2:7, 8).
- "Here we are—Parthians, Medes, Elamites, people from Mesopotamia, Judea, Cappadocia, Pontus, the province of Asia, Phrygia, Pamphylia, Egypt, and the areas of Libya around Cyrene, visitors from Rome (both Jews and converts to Judaism), Cretans, and Arabs [see map]. And we all hear these people *speaking in our own languages* about the wonderful things God has done!" (Acts 2:9–12).

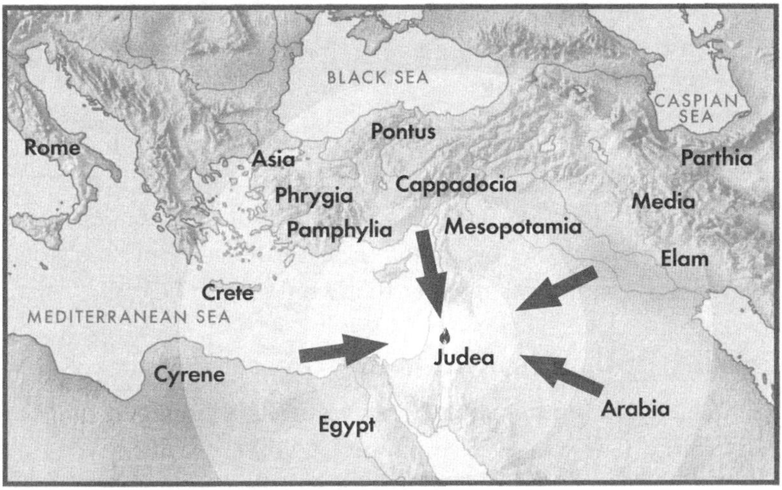

The cities and regions from which the pilgrims had come for Pentecost (see Acts 2:9–11).

Jesus had said, "You will receive power when the Holy Spirit comes on you; and *you will be my witnesses*" (Acts 1:8, NIV). The crowds heard the believers speaking "about the wonderful things God has done!" (Acts 2:11). Those who were Spirit baptised shared the gospel or good news of Jesus. It was to be a Spirit-led movement.

What does Spirit baptism look like? What did people see and hear? They saw people changed by Jesus, sharing about Jesus in a way they could understand.

The scope of this mission—Jerusalem, Judea, Samaria, and "to the ends of the earth" (Acts 1:8)—was confronting. Jesus' first followers were Jewish, with deeply entrenched national and religious prejudice toward Samaritans, gentiles, and those Jews who did not meet the requirements of the Torah. To invite people from these groups to become followers of Jesus required a radical shift of attitude, a fresh reading of Scripture and, in fact, the direct intervention of the Spirit.

So, what does Spirit baptism look like? What did people see and hear? They saw people changed by Jesus, sharing about Jesus in a way they could understand. The evidence of Spirit baptism was the disciples' empowerment to witness to the good news of their resurrected Saviour in a manner that would reach hearts.

Spirit baptism happens at conversion

Receiving this empowerment to witness is integral to our conversion. This is made clear in the only other teaching scripture about Spirit baptism. Almost 25 years after Pentecost, in the midst of counsel about the abuse of tongues-speaking in Corinth, Paul wrote:

> Some of us are Jews, some are Gentiles, some are slaves, and some are free. But we have all been baptised into one body by one Spirit, and we all share the same Spirit (1 Corinthians 12:13).[11]

Although in conflict with each other, Paul appealed to the Corinthian believers to consider their standing and unity in Christ. He did not say we shall be, or may be, or ought to be—but "we *were* all baptised by one Spirit" (1 Corinthians 12:13, NIV). Through Spirit baptism they had all become members of the body of Christ.

It was an accomplished reality for all believers—integral to conversion—even though they were "acting just like people of the world" (1 Corinthians 3:4).

There are no conversions without Spirit baptism

This was true on Pentecost day, and it is also true of all conversion experiences today. Spirit baptism is not a later extra or *second blessing*, which is the privilege of only some believers (see Appendix C). There is no conversion without Spirit baptism and no power for witness.

We are privileged to live in the Spirit's time!

The Holy Spirit came on the day of Pentecost. Spirit baptism that day was a once-for-all-time historical outpouring. It was "an event comparable in magnitude to the resurrection of Jesus Christ."[12] Just as Jesus died and rose once, so the Spirit came on Pentecost—never to leave. And just as Jesus was born by the Spirit's miracle-working power, so the body of Christ (the church) was born by the Spirit at Pentecost. And the Spirit's presence is the guarantee that the promise of salvation is not only for those of a certain race, gender or status—but is available to all.

EMPOWERED

Read Acts 1:1–2:47.

1. Reflect on what you have discovered about Holy Spirit baptism. List your key insights:

    -
    -
    -
    -

2. Some fear Spirit baptism. It might be concern about being manipulated or a fear of change—changed lives and churches. What concerns do you have?

3. Holy Spirit baptism was Jesus' anointing for ministry. What does it mean for you? How does Spirit baptism change our relationship with God and others?

CHAPTER 5

SURPRISED BY THE SPIRIT

Since the explosive growth of Pentecostalism in the latter half of the 20th century, many have associated speaking in tongues—or *glossolalia*—with Spirit baptism. In the 1970s and 1980s, Pentecostalism "rattled the gates"[1] of historic denominations, with Catholic, Protestant, evangelical, conservative and liberal congregations alike experiencing outbursts of tongues-speaking. This brought neo-Pentecostalism, then called charismatic renewal, to church life. It has been seen as the third force of Christianity—first Roman Catholicism, then the Protestant Reformation, and in the 20th century, the Charismatic movement.

Today the excitement has waned but that is largely because the charismatic renewal agenda is now widely accepted within Christianity. With this as the new normal, it is counter-cultural to even ask questions. But in our journey to know, be filled and empowered by the Spirit, it is important to ask: Is tongues-speaking now the evidence that one has experienced Spirit baptism? And is a *second blessing* of the Spirit biblical—the idea common in holiness or charismatic churches that we need an extra experience of the Spirit that is separate and additional to His work for our salvation? (See also Appendix C.)

In the light of the New Testament and church history, these are important questions.

The promise of Spirit baptism fulfilled again

As we saw in Chapter 4, the prophecies of Spirit baptism pointed to Pentecost day. The events of that day marked the beginning of the Spirit's era and the birth of the Christian church. Many pilgrims were "bewildered" or "completely amazed" (Acts 2:6, 7) by the Spirit's arrival. But note that it was the pilgrims who heard the 120 believers speaking in foreign languages who were "amazed and perplexed" (Acts 2:12)—not the believers themselves. It was what the Spirit did afterwards that amazed the believers. And what He did provides lessons that help us better understand His role today.

It was what the Spirit did afterwards that amazed the believers.

The first of these surprising experiences involved Samaritans. When persecution erupted following Stephen's martyrdom, Philip escaped to Samaria, where crowds accepted the good news of Jesus and were baptised in His name. However, with such intense hatred between them, it was difficult for Jerusalem's Jewish believers to accept that the Samaritans were following the same Messiah. Peter and John were sent to investigate:

> When they arrived, they prayed for the new believers there that they might receive the Holy Spirit, because the Holy Spirit had not yet come on any of them; they had simply been baptised in the name of the Lord Jesus. Then Peter and John placed their hands on them, and they received the Holy Spirit (Acts 8:15–17).

It was like a special Pentecost for the Samaritans. The Spirit did not need to wait for Peter and John to travel into the area, but He did—so that leaders of the Jewish believers could be with the Samaritan believers to experience this outpouring upon them. The message was unequivocal: there is one Saviour, one Spirit and one *body* of believers.

The second experience where Spirit baptism is specifically mentioned was even more confronting for the Jewish believers as it involved gentiles coming to faith. An "angel of God" instructed the Italian centurion Cornelius, at Caesarea, to call for Peter. The apostle arrived, and while speaking of Jesus' crucifixion and resurrection:

> The Holy Spirit fell upon all who were listening to the message. The Jewish believers who came with Peter were amazed that the gift of the Holy Spirit had been poured out on the gentiles, too. For they heard them speaking in other tongues and praising God.
>
> Then Peter asked, "Can anyone object to their being baptised, now that they have received the Holy Spirit just as we did?" So he gave orders for them to be baptised in the name of Jesus Christ (Acts 10:44–48).

Peter was as surprised as anyone that the Spirit had intervened. When news of this reached Jerusalem, the reaction was harsh. Jewish believers were swift in their criticism, "You entered the home of gentiles and even ate with them!" (Acts 11:3). Peter was forced to defend his visit to this gentile household at the heart of paganism and oppression, explaining:

> As I began to speak . . . the Holy Spirit fell on them, just as he fell on us at the beginning. Then I thought of the Lord's words when he said, 'John baptised with water, but you will be baptised with [in] the Holy Spirit.' And since God gave these gentiles the same gift he gave us when we believed in the Lord Jesus Christ, who was I to stand in God's way? (Acts 11:15–17).

Amazed, but with their objections answered, the Jewish believers in Jerusalem "began praising God," concluding, "God has also given the gentiles the privilege of repenting of their sins and receiving eternal life" (Acts 11:18). They had received the same Spirit. And while the struggles over national, racial, status and gender discrimination were to persist—and still do in the Christian church—this experience was their tipping point for mission.[2] The promises of the new covenant—salvation and Spirit baptism—were for all, even for the gentiles.

As well as Samaritans and gentile Italians coming to faith, there are three other conversion stories involving an arch-enemy and Jews from the fringes of society receiving Spirit baptism. These illustrate Peter's declaration on Pentecost day, "the promise is to you, to your children, and to those far away" (Acts 2:39). They show that forgiveness and Spirit baptism was available to a eunuch—someone sexually different—an Ethiopian who travelled to worship at the temple (see Acts 8:26–40); Saul, a bigoted Pharisaical persecutor (see Acts 9:1–31); and to diaspora Jews in Ephesus, Asia Minor (see Acts 19:1–10).

The Ethiopian accepted Jesus, was baptised and then "went on his way rejoicing" (Acts 8:39), indicating that he was Spirit-filled for his return to his home country. Saul was on his way to Damascus to interrogate and imprison believers when he was confronted by the risen Christ. Putting his trust in Jesus, he was "filled with the Holy Spirit" (Acts 9:17) before his water baptism and immediately began to speak of Jesus in the synagogue.

The third account is of Paul (originally Saul) arriving in Ephesus and observing a serious lack in the lives and witness of "several disciples" (Acts 19:1). This led him to ask the penetrating question, "Did you receive the Holy Spirit when you believed?" (Acts 19:2).[3] On learning they had received the baptism of John the Baptist but knew nothing of the Spirit, Paul shared more about Jesus:

> As soon as they heard this, they were baptised in the name of the Lord Jesus. Then when Paul laid his hands on them, the Holy Spirit came on them, and they spoke in other tongues and prophesied (Acts 19:5, 6).

They were not Christians being re-baptised, for they knew nothing of the Holy Spirit until this time. For the Ethiopian, Saul and these Ephesians, Spirit baptism was an anointing or commissioning for ministry as members of the church, or body of Christ.[4] There is no discrimination—all receive forgiveness through Jesus Christ, all are baptised by the same Spirit into the one body of believers, and all are anointed and empowered for disciple-making by that one Spirit.

Spirit baptism makes a huge difference

It is transformational. It represents the coming together of the two foundational historic truths of the Christian faith—Calvary and Pentecost. Jesus was crucified but is alive. He has ascended, but the Spirit brings the presence of Jesus and the Father to us. The Spirit's baptism affirms Calvary—and changes everything.

Spirit baptism makes the body of believers a new community—gentile and Jew, slave and free, female and male, with no economic, social or gender discrimination and no hierarchy. Spirit baptism makes us one body in Christ.

Speaking in other languages

Biblical writers used the Greek *glossa* to describe the physical organ, the tongue, as well as different languages, and also the act, content or results of speaking.[5] It surprises many who have sought a biblical basis for their experience to find that while it is recorded that thousands were converted, baptised and filled with the Spirit at Pentecost, few received the gift of speaking in unknown languages and ecstatic utterance is not reported at all in Acts.

The first occurrence of "other languages" on Pentecost day set the pattern for the others in Acts. While *new* to the apostles (see Mark 16:17), these were the *known* languages of the pilgrims at Pentecost—who exclaimed, "we all hear these people speaking in our own languages"—so no translation was needed (Acts 2:11). This gift is found three times in Acts—first among the 120 at Pentecost, then in the household of gentile Italians in Caesarea and among "about twelve" Jewish men in Ephesus—as *an* evidence of Holy Spirit baptism (see Acts 2:1–4; 10:44–48; 19:1–7).

The gift of tongues enabled believers to share the gospel in languages understandable to people who needed to hear about Jesus. The modern form of speaking in tongues that became popular in the latter part of the 20th century did not start that day.

It surprises many who have sought a biblical basis for the charismatic movement that . . . ecstatic utterance is not reported at all in the book of Acts.

In Mark 16:17, 18, Jesus listed signs that would accompany those who believed in Him: casting out demons, speaking in new languages, handling snakes, drinking poison without harm, and healing the sick. However, there is no evidence that Jesus expected all His followers to manifest all these signs. There are accounts of some sick being healed and demons cast out, one story involving a snake latching on to Paul's hand on Malta, but none of drinking poison in the New Testament. On Pentecost day, "the apostles performed many miraculous signs and wonders"—not the crowds—so it is clear that speaking in tongues and other signs are not required in conversion or our experience with God (see Acts 2:43).

There is no evidence that Jesus expected all His followers to manifest all these signs.

It is also a surprise to some that in the only two post-Pentecost experiences of tongues-speaking recorded in Acts—in Caesarea and Ephesus (see Acts 10:44–48, 19:1–7)—Holy Spirit baptism was not a second blessing but integral to conversion. There is no suggestion of a further distinct experience.

Conflict over spiritual gifts

About 25 years after Pentecost, jealousy and quarrelling (see 1 Corinthians 1:10–12, 3:1–4), gross immorality (see 1 Corinthians 5:1–13) and lawsuits (see 1 Corinthians 6:1–8) were tearing the Corinthian churches apart; even gathering for the Lord's Supper was doing "more harm than good" (see 1 Corinthians 11:17, 18). Open sin, lack of spiritual maturity and the abuse of spiritual gifts—especially tongues—were embarrassing the church. Some were claiming speaking in tongues as evidence of superior spirituality. Paul addressed their ignorance, scolding them for all coveting the same gift (see 1 Corinthians 12:1–31).

While Paul did not specifically define speaking in tongues or "other languages" as in Acts—where they are described as known languages and dialects—he used the same Greek word (see 1 Corinthians 12:10, 13:1, 14:2). He did not debate as to whether the gift was true or counterfeit, a known language or unintelligible sounds—even though glossolalia was found in other cultic religions, including in nearby Delphi. Rather, he challenged the abuse and taught how to relate to all spiritual gifts, in particular speaking in other languages.

Paul explained that there are different gifts. The Holy Spirit decides who gets which; they are not ours to demand. "We have all been baptised into one body by [in] one Spirit, and we all share the same Spirit" (1 Corinthians 12:13)—even those who do not speak in other languages.

The Spirit does not give one particular gift to all (see 1 Corinthians 12:4–31). And the spiritual fruits of "faith, hope and love" (1 Corinthians 13:13) are better than any other gifts—better than being an apostle, prophet, teacher or miracle worker; a greater witness than the gifts of healing, administration, tongues or interpretation (see 1 Corinthians 12:31–13:13).

Paul wrote, "Let love be your highest goal! But you should also desire the special abilities the Spirit gives—especially the ability to prophesy" (1 Corinthians 14:1). He commended the ability to speak in other languages or tongues, urging intelligible, understandable witness (see 1 Corinthians 14:1–25). "Be eager to prophesy," Paul urged, "and don't forbid speaking in tongues. But be sure that everything is done properly and in order" (1 Corinthians 14:39, 40).

Rather than causing division, as in Corinth, speaking in tongues is intended to strengthen, encourage, comfort, edify and instruct (see 1 Corinthians 14:3–6). Paul emphasised *understanding*—otherwise, "You might as well be talking into empty space . . . it won't strengthen the people who hear you" (1 Corinthians 14:9, 17).

"I thank God that I speak in tongues more than all of you," Paul told the Corinthians. "But in a church meeting I would rather speak five understandable words to help others than ten thousand words in an unknown language" (1 Corinthians 14:18, 19).

Paul's counsel for orderly worship (1 Corinthians 14:26–40)

- All are to be given opportunities to participate (verse 26).
- Spiritual gifts are to be used to strengthen the church (verse 26).
- If people are speaking in tongues (other languages), only two or three speak in a meeting, one at a time (verse 27).
- If there is no interpreter, remain silent (verses 27, 28).
- Words of prophecy are to be evaluated (verses 29–31).
- The gifts are under the person's control, so each can wait their turn (verse 32).

Spirit baptism in the post-Pentecost era

It surprises many to find that speaking in tongues is specifically mentioned in the New Testament so few times and that few believers filled with the Holy Spirit received this gift. While it was *an* evidence of Spirit baptism on the day of Pentecost, in Cornelius' home and in Ephesus, not all people filled with the Spirit spoke in other languages. Glossolalia was not synonymous with Spirit baptism.

In emphasising that "we have all been baptised into one body by [in] one Spirit, and we all share the same Spirit" (1 Corinthians 12:13), Paul made two things clear to the Corinthians. First, all believers have been Spirit-baptised: "You don't need to seek a Spirit-baptism as a post-conversion experience . . . if you are in Christ, you have already been Spirit-baptised!"[6] He wrote the same to the believers in Rome, reminding them "that those who do not have the Spirit of Christ living in them do not belong to him at all" (Romans 8:9). Second, believers who do not speak in other languages are still Spirit-baptised (1 Corinthians 12:12, 13). In fact, history reveals that tongues were not seen as the evidence of Spirit baptism until very recent times.

We must not let tongues-speaking distract from the significance of baptism in the Holy Spirit and our relationship with Him. Unfortunately, we can become so enamoured with this phenomenon—or fearful or concerned about it—that we neglect the Spirit Himself, *the* Gift.

His baptism or anointing is not to be feared. But neither is it a second blessing, bringing a superior Christian experience for selected people. Rather, Spirit baptism is integral to all conversions. It is always associated with water baptism, but not synonymous with it—for it is part of the process of conversion (see Acts 2:38, 39). As with believers in New Testament times, each person's journey will be different—some baptised by the Spirit before water baptism, some at the time of and some after (see Acts 8:14–17, 19:1–6). In addition, it is always anointing or commissioning into the priesthood of believers (see 1 Peter 2:9). Just as the Spirit came upon Jesus following His water baptism, so the Spirit anoints us for the ministry of disciple-making.

We must not let tongues-speaking distract from the significance of baptism in the Holy Spirit and our relationship with Him.

Holy Spirit baptism empowers us in our relationship with God and equips us to share the good news of Jesus and make disciples in our relational streams. With His anointing, He gives each of us abilities to make our witness effective—just as showers of rain bless and refresh, bringing life and growth.

EMPOWERED

Read 1 Corinthians 12:1–14:40.

1. What spiritual gift or ability do you believe God has given you? How are you using this gift to share your faith in Jesus?

2. Reflect on Paul's question to believers in Ephesus, "Did you receive the Holy Spirit when you believed?" (Acts 19:2).

3. Describe your anointing for witness at the time of your baptism.

4. With a group of friends, discuss your giftedness using the acronym SHAPE, and how this can be used to witness about Jesus Christ and share your journey with God:

   Spiritual gifts

   Heart passions

   Abilities

   Personality

   Experiences that have shaped you (both good and bad)

CHAPTER 6

RAIN

The prophet Joel forecast rain. He predicted "abundant showers" (Joel 2:23, NIV), resulting in great harvests.

Growing up in an old farmhouse and sleeping outdoors on the verandah connected us to the seasons. The dry thunderstorms at the end of hot summer days brought the danger of bushfires from lightning strikes that lit the night sky. The early winter rains created a din on the rusty corrugated tin roof, at times forcing us to retreat with our bedding to the hallway floor for a dry space.

Long before television, radio or even telephones came to our house, Mum was our resident weather forecaster. The surf of the Indian Ocean was almost three kilometres (2 miles) to the west, but if she heard the sea roaring, she predicted that rain was on its way. And if swarms of flying ants headed past on their way inland that was certain confirmation. How? I have no idea, but it seemed Mum was often correct in her predictions.

However, even as a boy, when I heard Dad read Joel's prophecy, it seemed to me that the prophet had an edge on Mum's predictions, for his forecast was prefaced with, "The Lord says" (Joel 2:12)—and, although Mum had strong faith, we knew she didn't speak with that authority!

On Pentecost day, the apostle Peter announced, "What Joel predicted centuries ago is here. It's raining" (Acts 2:16, my paraphrase).

The Spirit awakens life

As rain brings new life to dry dead seeds, with the moisture expanding them until they burst with new shoots, so we who are "dead" are awakened to "life" by the Spirit. This happens as the Spirit draws us into fellowship with Jesus (see Ephesians 2:1, 4, 5). That is what happened on the day of Pentecost. As Peter told the crowds the story of Jesus' crucifixion and resurrection, his "words pierced their hearts" and they cried out, "What should we do?" (Acts 2:37). Peter's response was:

> Each of you must repent of your sins and turn to God, and be baptised in the name of Jesus Christ for the forgiveness of your sins. Then you will receive the gift of the Holy Spirit (Acts 2:38).

This is sometimes called *regeneration*. Paul wrote that "even though we were dead because of our sins, he gave us life [or made us alive, NIV]" (Ephesians 2:4). And to Titus he wrote, "[Jesus] saved us through the washing of *regeneration and renewing* of the Holy Spirit" (Titus 3:5, footnote). Note how Paul explained this for us:

> He generously poured out the Spirit upon us through Jesus Christ our Saviour. Because of his grace he made us right in his sight and gave us confidence that we will inherit eternal life (Titus 3:6, 7).

Adam's sin resulted in complete ruin and separation from God. The 4th-century monk Pelagius (c360–418 AD) had the idea that sin only *tainted* us and that we can obey God to earn forgiveness and eternal life by our natural free-will, without the Spirit's aid. Sorry, that is not how it is! Without the Spirit's activity to awaken us to our need, we can't even start this journey—and the Spirit can only do this for us because of what Jesus Christ our Saviour did. It's never our work!

The Spirit awakens life in us, then:

The Spirit convicts us. Jesus explained, "when he [the Spirit] comes, he will convict the world of its sin, and of God's righteousness, and of the coming judgment" (John 16:8).

The Spirit converts us. We often refer to conversion as believing or being "born again" (John 3:3), so the fact that it is the Spirit who awakens us to salvation when we believe can be overlooked. Conversion is a gift from God (see Ephesians 2:8–10).

Jesus said to Nicodemus, "I tell you the truth, unless you are born again, you cannot see the Kingdom of God. . . . I assure you, no-one can enter the Kingdom of God without being born of water and the Spirit" (John 3:3, 5). As a Jewish teacher, Nicodemus would have been familiar with water and the Spirit as Old Testament symbols of renewal and cleansing. Describing His new-covenant restoration of Israel, God said through Ezekiel:

> I will sprinkle clean water on you, and you will be clean. Your filth will be washed away, and you will no longer worship idols. And I will give you a new heart, and I will put a new spirit in you. I will take out your stony, stubborn heart and give you a tender, responsive heart. And I will put my Spirit in you so that you will follow my decrees and be careful to obey my regulations" (Ezekiel 36:25–27; compare Isaiah 32:14–17, 44:3; Joel 2:28, 29).

Christ's point was unmistakable: without the spiritual washing or cleansing of the Holy Spirit, no-one can enter God's kingdom. The Spirit draws us to repentance, faith and conversion. The conversions on Pentecost day (see Acts 2:38, 39), of Saul (see Acts 9:17, 18), in Cornelius' home (see Acts 10:44–46, 11:15–17) and in Ephesus (see Acts 19:1–7), are all described in terms of receiving and being filled with the Spirit.

When we see conversion as a Holy Spirit event, we are challenged to then take another look at baptism—for conversion and baptism are when we receive the gift of the Spirit. Spirit baptism is part of the package of salvation. We are anointed by the Spirit and baptised into the body of Christ.

The Spirit baptises us

It was at the time of His baptism in water that Jesus was anointed or baptised with the Spirit, and this is to be our experience too. "This is what makes baptism what it is," says Richard Rice, "—the transforming entrance of the Holy Spirit into our lives."[1] Baptism is devalued when the two—water and Spirit—are separated. If we are simply immersed in water, we are not changed. We get wet and it doesn't hurt us, but it doesn't change us! This is not everything that baptism should be. When baptised in water *and the Spirit*, our lives are transformed—and there is no need for a second blessing, as some claim.

It has been my privilege to participate in many baptisms. Few have been mass baptisms, for which there is no New Testament example. As mentioned in Chapter 4, even the 3000 people baptised and added to the church on Pentecost day would have been baptised in homes around the city and adjacent to the temple steps, for there was no nearby river, lake or sea for a mass service.[2] I don't wish to devalue the meaning of baptism for those who have been baptised *en-masse*, but baptism is too important for new disciples to be nameless, unrecognised and just a number.

The Spirit is ready to baptise believers. The writer of Hebrews considered baptism to be one of the "basic teachings about Christ," along with repentance, faith in God, "the laying on of hands, the resurrection of the dead, and eternal judgment" (Hebrews 6:1, 2). In fact, he used the plural *baptisms*, to draw attention to the need for baptism by water *and* the Spirit. It is Spirit baptism that makes the complete "one baptism," of which Paul wrote to the Ephesians believers (see Ephesians 4:5).

So how are we baptised by the Spirit? Unfortunately, although the Spirit's anointing and presence is a prominent New Testament feature, few Bible studies used for induction into church membership mention His baptism. Spirit baptism is intergral to conversion, and the following journey celebrates His baptism:

1. Introduce Jesus and His Spirit through the Bible. People need to hear the story of Jesus' life, death and resurrection, and understand the plan of salvation. The *Discovery Bible Reading* process is a good way to do this. It is a simple journey that anyone can facilitate, which involves reading through books of the Bible—starting with the gospels—with friends or colleagues (see Appendix A for an outline). As people learn of Jesus, they are also introduced to the Holy Spirit. The gospel of John covers all fundamentals of the Christian faith and includes Jesus' talks about the Spirit. When people are convicted to put their faith in Jesus, you are seeing the work of the Spirit's baptism.

2. At each baptism—whether in a river, mountain stream, lake, baptistry or font, swimming pool, the sea or farm dam—gather those baptised in "the name of the Father, and the Son, and the Holy Spirit" for prayer, just as Jesus prayed at the Jordan (Matthew 28:19; see Luke 3:21, 23).

3. Surrounded by believers who lay their hands on their heads or shoulders, together with family and friends who are not yet believers, spend time in simple direct prayer rejoicing in the Holy Spirit's anointing or baptism. This is entirely consistent with the evangelism of the New Testament.

I have heard those anointed share, "The Spirit filled me with peace," "He filled me with joy," "It was amazing. It was like the Holy Spirit embraced me with the warmth of God's love" and "He filled me with an inner assurance that I am secure in Christ." There may be more dramatic gifts, but faces light up, the church or body of believers enriched, and unbelieving family and friends convicted as lives are changed and new disciples are empowered for life and ministry.

Empowered for living

This complete view of baptism in water and Spirit provides fresh perspectives. Baptism is not graduation from a course of doctrinal studies but a transformative new beginning. Let's consider some of the ways that the Spirit empowers the life of a Christian:

The Spirit empowers our witness

At first it might seem strange to discuss witnessing before the Spirit's continuing work in us. However, I want to avoid the error of suggesting that we must reach a certain level of holiness before we make disciples. As soon as Jesus made new disciples, He involved them in disciple-making.

The Spirit redefines mission. He led Philip to Samaritans and the Ethiopian eunuch, and Peter to the household of an Italian gentile. Be prepared to be led to people you don't consider your type. This is a transformative journey. There will be crazy twists and turns. For Jesus, the Spirit first led Him into the wilderness. Don't be surprised if the devil turns up to throw every temptation and distraction before you. But don't be discouraged. Sharing faith transforms and invigorates our lives, for we are cooperating with the Spirit. We are drawn into the inner circle of the Trinity as co-workers.

The Spirit also gives us spiritual gifts for service. Writing to the Corinthian churches to correct their abuse of the gifts, Paul referred to a variety of "special abilities" (1 Corinthians 12:1) that the Spirit gives. There are many, and when He fills us with His presence, He gives to each as He chooses, for He knows what is needed (see 1 Corinthians 12:4–11).

The focus is not on the gift or ability, but on the service. Preoccupation with the gift distracts from the message and its benefits for others.

The focus is not on the gift or ability but on the service. Preoccupation with the gift distracts from the message and its benefits for others. Whatever dramatic manifestations or miracles might accompany the Spirit, His purpose is to empower and equip us to lead others to Christ (see James 5:13–20).

Each will be given "different gifts for doing certain things well" (Romans 12:6). These gifts might include speaking for God, serving, teaching, encouraging, giving, leading or showing kindness. Paul encouraged believers to use their gifts to the best of their ability:

> So if God has given you the ability to prophesy, speak out with as much faith as God has given you. If your gift is serving others, serve them well. If you are a teacher, teach well. If your gift is to encourage others, be encouraging. If it is giving, give generously. If God has given you leadership ability, take the responsibility seriously. And if you have a gift for showing kindness to others, do it gladly (Romans 12:6–8).

When writing to the believers in Ephesus, a church that was a mission hub for witnessing to the surrounding region (see note under Empowered, at the end of the chapter), Paul reminded the churches of the source of spiritual gifts:

> When he ascended to the heights, he . . . gave gifts to his people. . . . Now these are the gifts Christ gave to the church: the apostles, the prophets, the evangelists, and the pastors and teachers (Ephesians 4:8, 11).

These have been called the APEPT gifts.[3] All are called to participate in witnessing, with these five roles operating and embraced by each congregation or fellowship:

Apostles: those sent to gather new disciples.

Prophets: those with spiritual sensitivity or discernment.

Evangelists: those with skills to invite people to follow Jesus.

Pastors: those with compassion and care, as shepherds.

Teachers: those with clear skills to instruct and explain God's plan.

The purpose of these gifts in the church is clear:

> Their responsibility is to equip God's people to do his work [for works of service, NIV] and build up the church, the body of Christ. This will continue until we all come to such unity in our faith and knowledge of God's Son that we will be mature in the Lord, measuring up to the full and complete standard of Christ (Ephesians 4:12, 13).

Participation by all grows a healthy fellowship that is "full of love" (Ephesians 4:16) and no longer immature and tossed about by every strange doctrinal theory. The Spirit provides the gifts and empowers our witness, and all believers mature in faith (see Ephesians 4:14–16; compare 1 Thessalonians 1:4–6; 1 Peter 1:10–12).

The Spirit lives in us, sealing us for redemption

When we choose to believe in Jesus, trust our lives to Him and witness to our faith by being baptised, the Holy Spirit makes His home in us—and in this way, Jesus said that He and the Father would make their home in us too (see John 14:17, 20, 23). God identifies us as His, and we become "the temple of the Holy Spirit" (1 Corinthians 6:19; see Ephesians 1:13, 5:18–21). Living within, the Spirit *seals* us for redemption:

> Now it is God who makes both us and you stand firm in Christ. He anointed us, set his seal of ownership on us, and put his Spirit in our hearts as a deposit, guaranteeing what is to come (2 Corinthians 1:21, 22, NIV).

The Spirit is God's guarantee that He will give us the inheritance He promised and that He has purchased us to be His own people (Ephesians 1:14; compare 2 Corinthians 5:5).

This "seal of the living God" is very special—marking those who are redeemed by Jesus and filled with the Spirit, contrasted with the efforts of the evil one to enslave and mark us as His (see Revelation 7:1–3, 14:1; 13:17).

The Spirit changes us

Paul wrote to the Ephesians, explaining that the Spirit transforms us and gives us "mighty inner strength," filling us "with all the fullness of life and power that comes from God" (Ephesians 3:16, 19). He exclaimed, "Now all glory to God, who is able, through his mighty power at work within us, to accomplish infinitely more than we might ask or think" (Ephesians 3:20; compare Titus 3:3–7).

When we choose "to let the Holy Spirit guide [our] lives" (Galatians 5:16), He changes our relationships with our families, friends, work associates, neighbours and fellow believers. Living in us, the Spirit produces fruit that transforms all these relationships with "love, joy, peace, patience, kindness, goodness, faithfulness, gentleness and self-control" (Galatians 5:22, 23).

The Spirit makes us holy

In God's sight, the Spirit has made us holy. The apostle Peter wrote to "God's chosen people" (1 Peter 1:1) across Asia Minor (modern Turkey):

> God the Father knew you and chose you long ago, and his Spirit has made you holy [through the sanctifying work of the Spirit, NIV]. As a result, you have obeyed him and have been cleansed by the blood of Jesus Christ (1 Peter 1:2).

This is the most amazing reality. The Trinity lives and works within us, and "the Lord—who is the Spirit—makes us more and more like him as we are changed into his glorious image" (2 Corinthians 3:18; compare 1 Corinthians 6:19, 20; James 4:5).

In God's sight, we are clean—justified (declared right with God) and sanctified (made holy in His sight)—"in the name of the Lord Jesus Christ and by the Spirit of our God" (1 Corinthians 6:11, NIV). By the Spirit, we experience progressive growth for obedience to Jesus Christ. What assurance is ours! This is not our work—but the Spirit's.

Streams of living water will flow from within!

Following His baptism in the Jordan, Jesus was praying when "the Holy Spirit, in bodily form, descended on him like a dove" and the Father's voice was heard declaring Jesus to be His Son (see Luke 3:21, 22). Many years later, Peter explained:

> God anointed Jesus of Nazareth with the Holy Spirit and with power. Then Jesus went around doing good and healing all who were oppressed by the devil, for God was with him (Acts 10:38).

He came to the Jordan as Jesus and left as the Christ, anointed with the Spirit to make disciples. With this anointing, He "began his public ministry" (Luke 3:23). In the same way, our Spirit baptism is not a sprinkling but an outpouring that overwhelms or immerses us with His presence. And with the Spirit filling us, He flows from within us to refresh others.

Bringing it all together—the Spirit gives life

Think about it. The Spirit awakens us to spiritual things, convicts and converts us. He baptises us, living in us, changing, sanctifying and empowering us. The Spirit gives life.

In "Rediscovering the Spirit-filled life," Richard Rice writes:

> If the Spirit's essential function is to give life, then we should think of sanctification as the enrichment and enhancement of our lives. In other words, to grow in grace is to become more and more alive. Too often, we think of sanctification in negative terms. It involves giving up more and more—overcoming bad habits, eliminating sins from our lives, avoiding transgression, and so on. But a Spirit-centred view of salvation turns things around.

Then Rice sums up the essence of such a Spirit-filled life:

> The Spirit enters our lives not to take, but to give. Sanctification means gaining something, not losing something. In the final analysis, sanctification is not

> what God wants from us, but what God wants for us. It is the richest, fullest life possible. That's what life in the Holy Spirit is.[4]

Without Pentecost and the Holy Spirit, there would be no awareness of salvation. In Jesus and His Spirit, we have eternal life.

Without Calvary and the resurrection, there would be no salvation. Without Pentecost and the Holy Spirit, there would be no awareness of salvation. Like refreshing showers of rain in season, in Jesus and His Spirit, we have eternal life.

EMPOWERED

Read the book of Ephesians. Choose an easy-to-read translation such as the New Living Translation, maybe get a hot drink, find a quiet spot and read the entire letter in one sitting.

Ephesians is one of Paul's last letters, written about 61–62 AD from imprisonment in Rome to God's people at Ephesus. Paul had cultivated an agile base there for equipping disciples—a mission hub. Different to the mission stations or ministry centres of the 19th and 20th centuries, Paul worked quickly to equip new believers. They then returned to their home cities across the Roman province of Asia Minor to multiply disciples and household churches through their natural relational streams (families, friends, work and community relationships).

1. As you read, identify the activities of the Spirit that Paul writes of and reflect on your journey and the Spirit's work for you:

- How has He awakened or regenerated you?

- How has He convicted or convinced you?

- How has He converted you?

- How has He baptised you into the body of Christ?

- How has He lived in you as the guarantee of salvation?

- How has He given you gifts and engaged you for service?

- How has He filled you?

- How has He empowered you, giving inner strength for life and witness?

2. How did you feel as you read this letter and thought of Paul writing from prison? What might have been the emotions of the believers in Ephesus, with whom Paul had lived and worked tirelessly while under constant threat?

3. Reflect on God's amazing grace for you, and what it means to know that every single aspect of your conversion and spiritual journey—from having your spiritual interest awakened to your sanctification or spiritual maturity—is the work of the Holy Spirit, yours as a gift of God's grace. Describe what this means to you, perhaps by writing a short letter to God.

4. There is "one baptism" (Ephesians 4:5)—in water and Spirit. In what way were you prepared for the Spirit's baptism? What difference did it make?

CHAPTER 7

AUTUMN AND SPRING RAIN

Peter explained the outpouring of the Holy Spirit on the day of Pentecost in the light of Joel's forecast of autumn and spring rain, quoting, "'In the last days,' God says, 'I will pour out my Spirit upon all people'" (Acts 2:17).

Being in the northern hemisphere, the autumn rains were expected across Israel and Judea in late September to November. These early rains germinated the seed as it was planted and gave growth. The later spring rains, just before Passover in March to April, filled out the grain for harvest by Pentecost time, and provided moisture to mature the olives, grapes and other fruit by the Feast of Shelters in late summer.

Once the Spirit fell on Pentecost, His rain kept coming—refreshing, anointing and empowering the lives and witness of the growing body of Christ. There would be prophecies, visions and signs, "but everyone who calls on the name of the Lord will be saved" (Acts 2:21).

Throughout the first century, the Spirit's rain fell—poured out and filling God's people. These terms—*poured out* and *filled*—were used to describe Spirit baptism on Pentecost day, as well as the continuing showers of New Testament times (see Acts 2:4, 33; 4:31). This is as Peter declared on Pentecost: "This promise [of forgiveness of sin in Jesus and the gift of the Holy Spirit] is to you, to your children, and to those far away [to the gentiles, footnote]—all who have been called by the Lord our God" (Acts 2:39).

Later, when an astounded crowd rushed to the temple colonnades to see a well-known crippled beggar now healed, Peter "saw his opportunity" (Acts 3:12) to speak of the resurrected Jesus—and again he promised ongoing refreshing rain. He also spoke of Jesus' return:

> Now repent of your sins and turn to God, so that your sins may be wiped away. Then times of refreshment will come from the presence of the Lord, and he will again send you Jesus, your appointed Messiah. For he must remain in heaven until the time for the final restoration of all things, as God promised long ago through his holy prophets (Acts 3:19–21).

Ongoing refreshing rain

The evidence of the Spirit's presence through New Testament times—to the end of the first century—is fascinating to observe. For example, when the need arose to administer a food program for poorer believers, no doubt because the social support and resources of the temple were now denied followers of the Way, people "*full of the Spirit* and wisdom" (Acts 6:3) were put in charge (see Acts 6:1–7).

One of the men chosen to administer the food program was Stephen, "a man full of God's grace and power" who "performed amazing miracles and signs among the people"—and who *spoke* by the Spirit (see Acts 6:8, 10). He was brought before the Sanhedrin, falsely accused of blasphemy (see Acts 6:11-14). They were enraged when, "full of the Holy Spirit," Stephen declared that he saw Jesus "standing in the place of honour at God's right hand" (Acts 7:55, 56). He was dragged from the city and killed (see Acts 7:57–60).

Another instance demonstrating the ongoing presence of the Holy Spirit was when Ananias was sent to Saul (later known as the apostle Paul) in Damascus:

> He laid his hands on him and said, "Brother Saul, the Lord Jesus, who appeared to you on the road, has sent me so that you might regain your sight and *be filled with the Holy Spirit*." Instantly something like scales fell from Saul's eyes, and he regained his sight. Then he got up and was baptised.... And immediately he began preaching about Jesus in the synagogues, saying, "He is indeed the Son of God!" (Acts 9:17, 18, 20, emphasis added)

Barnabas, a Levite from Cyprus, was another man the Bible points to as enjoying the presence of the Holy Spirit. He was described as "a good man, *full of the Holy Spirit* and strong in faith" (Acts 11:24, emphasis added). With believers scattered from Jerusalem by persecution, the gospel was taken to Antioch in Syria where people of different ethnicities believed in Jesus. Barnabas was sent to encourage them (see Acts 11:19–24).

These are just a few examples of people that the Holy Spirit empowered following Pentecost. Similar to the experience on the day of Pentecost, the Holy Spirit gave these people a special ability to speak of the wonders of God seen in the death and resurrection of Jesus. The rain continued to fall.

The showers spread to the gentile world

Sometimes showers of rain can be scattered or intermittent, benefiting only some. But not so with the showers of the Spirit. His activity and blessing were for all. The Spirit sent Paul and Barnabas on their first missionary journey to Cyprus and southern Galatia, filling them and the new gentile believers "with joy and with the Holy Spirit" (Acts 13:52).

In his letter to these new gentile believers in Galatia, Paul wrote:

> Through Christ Jesus, God has blessed the Gentiles with the same blessing he promised to Abraham, so that we who are believers might receive the promised Holy Spirit through faith.... For you are all children of God through faith in Christ Jesus (Galatians 3:14, 26; compare 3:2, 5, 4:6).

Paul also wrote to the Galatians:

> So I say, let the Holy Spirit guide your lives... the Spirit gives us desires that are the opposite of what the sinful nature desires (Galatians 5:16, 17).
>
> But the Holy Spirit produces this kind of fruit in our lives: love, joy, peace, patience, kindness, goodness, faithfulness, gentleness and self-control (Galatians 5:22, 23).
>
> Since we are living by the Spirit, let us follow the Spirit's leading in every part of our lives... those who live to please the Spirit will harvest everlasting life from the Spirit (Galatians 5:25; 6:8).

At the Jerusalem consultation, which was called to discuss whether the gospel was for Jews and gentiles alike, Peter reflected on God's activity in the home of Cornelius: "God... confirmed that he accepts gentiles by giving them the Holy Spirit, just as he did to us" (Acts 15:8). And Barnabas and Paul "told about the miraculous signs and wonders God had done through them among the Gentiles" on their recent journey (Acts 15:12).

In the same way that He worked in the lives of the gentile believers in Galatia, the Holy Spirit swept across province after province with showers of blessing. Paul's second journey was also guided by the Spirit, as was his third to Ephesus where "God gave Paul the power to do unusual miracles" (Acts 19:11). He then "felt compelled by the Holy Spirit" (Acts 19:21) to visit Macedonia and Greece, before being "bound" or "irresistibly" drawn "to go to Jerusalem" (Acts 20:22) before his planned mission to Rome and Spain.

The Holy Spirit swept across province after province with showers of blessing.

All the New Testament epistles clearly indicate that the Holy Spirit continued to be poured out after Pentecost, filling and empowering all believers to witness to their faith in Jesus and multiply disciples and churches. Paul reminded the believers in Thessalonica that "when we brought you the Good News, it was not only with words but also with *power*, for *the Holy Spirit gave you full assurance* that what we said was true" (1 Thessalonians 1:5, emphasis added; compare 2 Thessalonians 2:13).

Paul constantly referred the Corinthian believers, with their internal divisions, back to their need for the Spirit. For example, they needed to remember that:

- "Only those who are spiritual can understand what the Spirit means" (1 Corinthians 2:14).
- They were His temples (see 1 Corinthians 3:16, 17; 6:19, 20).
- It was the Spirit alone who "decides which gift each person should have" (1 Corinthians 12:11).
- They had "all been baptised into one body by one Spirit" (1 Corinthians 12:13).

In his epistle to the Romans, written from Corinth in the winter of 56–57 AD, Paul wrote his masterpiece on life in the Spirit (see Romans 8:1–9:3). He also wrote of spiritual gifts (see Romans 12:6–8).

Even in his final letters, the theme continues. The letters to the Philippians, Ephesians and Colossians were sent from a prison in Rome in 61–62 AD. He reminded the Philippians of their "fellowship together in the Spirit" (Philippians 2:1; compare 2 Corinthians 13:14). Like a down-payment or deposit, he told the Ephesians, "when you believed in Christ, he identified you as his own by giving you the Holy Spirit. . . . The Spirit is God's guarantee that he will give us the inheritance he promised and that he has purchased us to be his own people" (Ephesians 1:13, 14; compare 2 Corinthians 1:22, 5:5). He urged them to "be filled with the Holy Spirit" (Ephesians 5:18).

Paul's letters to Titus and Timothy—and perhaps Hebrews—were his last, written as late as 63–64 AD from Rome's Mammertime prison just prior to his execution. He encouraged Timothy to "fan into flames the spiritual gift God gave you when I laid my hands on you" (2 Timothy 1:6). Urging him to be a faithful teacher, Paul wrote, "Through the power of the Holy Spirit who lives within us, carefully guard the precious truth that has been entrusted to you" (2 Timothy 1:14).

In the years after Pentecost, the Spirit's presence, anointing and indwelling empowerment were a constantly falling rain.

But did the showers of the Spirit cease?

By the end of the apostolic period, the Spirit's presence seemed but a drizzle. It was not that the Spirit went away but controversy and the wrong use of sacraments to secure salvation pushed Him aside. As the church became increasingly political, attention was distracted from Him, His inspiration, grace and empowerment.[1]

While Tertullian (155–220? AD) was the first to use the term *Trinity*, the baptismal formula Jesus gave (see Matthew 28:18, 19) and the early doxologies in the epistles (see 2 Corinthians 13:14) breathed "a Trinitarian spirit."[2] However, when the apostles died, the Spirit's supernatural presence and gifts were neglected.

Into this vacuum, in the early to mid-second century, arose Montanus of Mysia on the southern-central coast of Turkey. He claimed that the prophetic gift had returned to him. He also claimed that a level of holiness not even achieved by the apostles was now available and that his "utterances, ecstasies and prophecies" were to be accepted as evidence of the Spirit's anointing.[3] As you can imagine, while his views spread quite widely, they were not received by the church. In fact, many Christians became wary of any revelation other than from the Scriptures for centuries to come.

Then, in the third and fourth centuries, two competing ideas were born, both undermining the co-equal relationship of the Spirit with the Father and Son. In the third century, it was Sabellianism or modalism, the idea that there is one God who appears in three modes—like three faces on the one person. In the fourth century, Arianism was promulgated, the idea that both Jesus and the Spirit are subordinate to the Father. Arianism teaches that the Father originated the Son by creating Him and that the Spirit was "the creature of a creature."[4]

Following Constantine's "conversion" in or about 312 AD, the Christian church moved from the margins of society to become the mainstream religion. But this was a time of raging and paralysing debate. Some people supported the co-equal eternal existence of the divine three. Others argued for Arianism, denying the divinity and eternal existence of both Jesus and the Spirit. Both sides sought the support of Constantine, literally warring against each other. The period between the First and Second General Councils of Nicea and Constantinople (325–381 AD) was particularly chaotic.

The acrimonious debate continued for centuries. This was fuelled in 589 AD at the Council of Toledo. While affirming the truth that the Spirit is of the Father (see John 15:26) and Son (see Galatians 4:6), the *filioque* statement—meaning, "and from the Son"—was inserted by the Western Church in an unauthorised and arbitrary way into the Nicene-Constantinopolitan creed. This was ultimately the flashpoint that caused the schism between the Eastern and Western branches of Christianity in 1054.[5]

While divergent theories about the Spirit persisted, the 16th-century Reformers believed the Holy Spirit to be co-equal and eternal with the Father and Son. And by the 18th century, with the focus on God's Word and salvation by God's grace alone, refreshing showers of the Spirit were falling across Europe and America.

End-time rain and holiness movements

The Great Awakening revivals of the 18th century were powerful times of Holy Spirit activity, with spiritual interest reaching fever-pitch during the Second Advent revivals of the early 19th-century. Centuries of spiritual drought separated the Spirit's outpouring at Pentecost from that time of dreams, visions and other dramatic manifestations.

End-time scenarios proliferated, with some predicting the time of Jesus' return and the end of the world. People thought "the last days" had come and were desperate to be ready to meet Jesus. Thousands turned to the churches.

This desperation gave birth to holiness movements with dramatic physical manifestations. The erratic second-century excesses of Montanus[6] were revived, with many seeking a level of holiness surpassing that of the apostles. There was shouting and people falling to the floor unable to arise, miracles, and ecstatic, gibberish-like speech.

Some believed it was the beginning of an apocalyptic latter rain of the Spirit, when the earth would be brightened with "his splendour" (see Revelation 18:1–4; compare Revelation 14:6–20; Ezekiel 43:1–4). Long centuries had passed since Peter's Pentecost announcement that Joel's vision of "autumn and springs rains" was being fulfilled (see Joel 2:18–32; compare Acts 2:14–40), which for some seemed to fit the idea of two seasons of rain (as illustrated below).

The Second Advent revivals involved people from many denominations, including Baptist, Methodist and Christian Connection churches. Among other denominations, the Seventh-day Adventist church was born in this intense spiritual environment of Advent revivalism. Early Adventists had charismatic experiences, such as visions, miracles, shouting and falling, as well as ecstatic tongues.[7] However, they soon learned that physical manifestations could not be relied upon as the ultimate evidence of the Spirit's baptism or filling. Some experiences proved to be genuine, while others were spurious—the result of excitement, manipulation or the influence of evil. It was clear that each needed to be tested thoroughly by Scripture.

It was an intense time of all-night prayer sessions and people crying out to God. In the mid-19th century, there was widespread ignorance in regard to disease. The concept of germs was unknown, night air was thought to be poisonous, poisons were

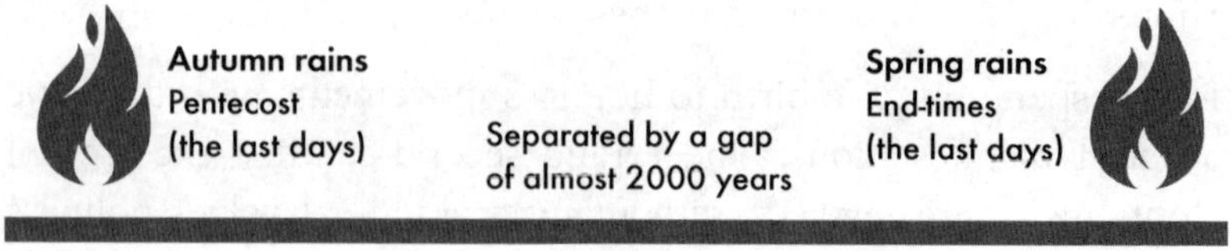

The Spirit's Pentecost activities were separated from His end-time activities.

prescribed as medication, blood was drained by physicians from patients with a fever, anaesthetics were unknown, surgery was crude and usually fatal. This meant that "almost any kind of sickness was an occasion for terror."[8] Healing miracles were relied upon and occurred frequently, but like all other manifestations of the Spirit these needed to be tested to see if they were genuine.

In this environment of earnest prayer and seeking to be prepared with a superior level of holiness for Jesus' second coming, the 4th-century heresies of Pelagius also reappeared. Pelagius had popularised the place of human will and effort in salvation. He took the position that Adam's sin had tainted but not completely ruined us, with salvation therefore within our reach without the Spirit's aid.[9] Those called semi-Pelagians conceded that our salvation starts with God's grace, but is dependent on human effort. This idea of cooperative effort was prominent in the holiness movements. It was accompanied by dramatic physical displays, which were seen as evidence of a second blessing of the Spirit and a superior level of holiness. For more detail, see Appendix C.

A potent mix—opportunities and dangers ahead

The revivals of the 18th and 19th centuries, with their preaching of various end-time scenarios and the urgent message to be ready for Christ's return, gave birth to an expanding movement of Christian mission, but there were dangers ahead, including:

- The pursuit of a level of holiness greater than that achieved by the apostles.
- Reliance on human effort in addition to God's grace to achieve this holiness.

- Believing that repentance and justification were not sufficient to be saved.

- Separating the Spirit's work of conversion from that of sanctification.

- Separating the "one baptism" into two disconnected experiences: first, water baptism; then a later Spirit baptism, referred to as a *second blessing*.

- Expecting that dramatic physical signs of miracles, shouting, ecstatic speech and falling down will always accompany the second-blessing or latter-rain—as some called it—outpouring of the Spirit.

Salvation is the free gift of God's grace and His Spirit—"from the beginnings of [our] conversion to the end of [our] perfection."[10] Our spiritual growth or maturity is the result of the "sanctifying work of the Spirit" (1 Peter 1:2, NIV). The apostle Paul challenged any suggestion that human effort can contribute in any way to our holiness or sanctification. He asked:

> What gives you the right to make such a judgment? What do you have that God hasn't given you? And if all you have is from God, why boast as though it were not a gift? (1 Corinthians 4:7).

We are entirely dependent on the Spirit's grace. If we trust our own efforts, we have no assurance of salvation. We grow "tired of wondering if we've worked enough, or repented enough, or trusted enough, to be saved . . . tired of the suspense of waiting until Christ comes to find out." And we seek "tangible evidence that we are right with God right now, that we are part of His kingdom today, in short, that we are really saved."[11]

In pursuing a superior level of holiness or last-generation righteousness, the good news of what Jesus has accomplished is set aside by our own works, often producing either despair or a judgmental spirit. We cannot achieve a greater degree of holiness in these end-times than the apostles in their day, for our holiness—justification and sanctification—like theirs, is equally the gift of God's grace.

This is what happened in Corinth. Some boasted of their holiness, touting the dramatic gift of tongues as the evidence, while being at the same time in conflict with their fellow believers, living immoral lives and neglecting the biblical purpose of the gifts. The apostle Paul challenged their claims of a defining superior gift, declaring, "There are different kinds of gifts, but the same Spirit . . . and he distributes them to each one, just as he determines" (1 Corinthians 12:4, 11, NIV).

Pursuing a dramatic exciting gift can distract from the Spirit Himself and from humble obedience to the Father's eternal will, commands and kingdom agenda.

Unfortunately, as in Corinth, pursuing a dramatic exciting gift can distract from the Spirit Himself and from humble obedience to the Father's eternal will, commands and kingdom agenda.

The surprise of latter rain

While not always acknowledged, the Spirit has been actively present in this world and in believers since Pentecost. Although there have been long centuries of spiritual drought, the Holy Spirit has never left. He has consistently anointed, filled and empowered faithfulness in living, mission and service.

The book of Revelation provides glimpses of an outpouring of the Spirit, accompanying God's very last calls of mercy before this world descends into total chaos and Jesus returns. With His call to "come away" or "come out" of Babylon, the earth brightens with "splendour" (Revelation 18:1–4; compare Revelation 14:6–20; Ezekiel 43:1–4). In Jesus' final message to John on Patmos, He gave the following invitation:

> The Spirit and the bride say, "Come!" Let anyone who hears this say, "Come!" Let anyone who is thirsty come. Let anyone who desires drink freely from the water of life (Revelation 22:17).

The warnings to come out of Babylon and to come to Jesus are urgent. The rain of the Spirit may be falling all around us and we may be unaware—surprised to have missed it. When we are not actively engaged in disciple-making and cultivating new faith communities, we can be blind to the Spirit's activity. It is like missing the showers of rain when we are cloistered away inside, instead of being out in the fields. By focusing on a future latter rain, a superior experience or a second blessing, we might miss His active presence now. The answer for our deep desire for assurance is found in looking to Jesus and living a Spirit-filled life now.

Enjoy the rain. Be refreshed. And, as a farmer in God's fields, facilitate the growth, harvest, and multiplication of disciples around you.

EMPOWERED

Read Revelation 1:1–3:22.

1. Observe the relationship of "the sevenfold [perfect] Spirit" with Jesus and the Father, and Jesus' call to hear Him (see

Revelation 2:7, 11, 17, 29; 3:6, 13, 22). What will you obey or apply personally, from what the Spirit said to these seven churches planted by Paul during his ministry in Ephesus (see Acts 18:1–10)?

2. Why do you think many seek dramatic manifestations of the Spirit? Reflect on these possible reasons, and consider others:
   - Doctrinal or theological fatigue, from over-emphasising dogmatic precision at the expense of experience.
   - Disillusionment with predictable, unsatisfying worship experiences in a world of slick, exciting, compact, fast-moving, stimulating entertainment.
   - Disconnection from God, with the pressures of life or lack of desire screening out time for Bible reading or meaningful times of family worship.
   - Desire for certainty or religious assurance, with dramatic manifestations thought to provide a visible demonstration or evidence of spiritual power and security.

3. What does it mean to you to experience the consistent daily refreshing of the early and latter rain of the Holy Spirit? How does His presence give assurance to you and empower your living and witness to the good news of salvation in Jesus?

4. In what ways does Spirit baptism cultivate and advance God's movement in your relational streams and challenge individualised truth and values?

CHAPTER 8

RIVERS FLOWING FROM WITHIN

> For the Scriptures declare, "Rivers of living water will flow from the heart of anyone who believes in me" (John 7:38, footnote).

It was a very dry season—with very little rain. A new well was needed close to the dairy, a humble structure that we more appropriately called the cowshed. We hand-milked a mixed herd, supplying milk to a nearby seaside caravan park and cream to the butter factory in town.

The decision for the new well had hardly been made when Steve Mitchell drove over the dry hills from the farm gate in his dilapidated canvas-topped (well, there were remnants of canvas there!) farm Land Rover, with his half a dozen dogs smiling from the back—perhaps pleased their 150-kilometre (90-mile) trip was over. There were no telephones or internet in those days, so maybe a telegram had been sent for help.

Steve was a rough, gruff man of few words but everyone said he had a heart of gold. He would always arrive unannounced. With a grunt of greeting, he sat on the verandah. His dogs and our blue-heeler cattle dog seemed delighted to catch up.

With few words, we then headed up the rise, along the hot black sandy path into a dry bush area of peppermint trees behind the cowshed. At this point, an older man who had retired to a property further south turned up too. George Barker was a stick of a man, always caring. Dad had possibly spoken to him at church.

Just to the east of the cowshed was a three-to-four-metre (10-to-12-foot) deep well that had been dug into the sand, some said 10 or more years earlier. It was dry. There had never been water. The men wandered over, looked in, and concluded, "No water there!"

Although only 10–12 years old at the time, my two brothers and I could have told them that without looking. We had peered in many times and climbed in a few times too, and we knew that whoever had dug there had found nothing but sand.

But just to the west of the cowshed, the men were more hopeful. We three boys were not so sure. The sand was just as hot to our bare toes, the flies were just as persistently annoying, and the dogs—well, they were off exploring the bush for rabbits, lizards or snakes.

The landscape in the region was dotted with caves and featured many underground streams. Although it looked to us like only hot, dry sand, after carefully surveying this part of our farm, these men were agreed—"There's water there!" Finally, they had a conference among the trees. "Yes, there are streams down there. One crossing from the south-east, another from the south, and a third, deeper down." It was then concluded that the lower stream was just above rock and that to get the best flow of water we would need to dig down six to eight metres (20 to 26 feet). I still don't understand how they knew, but we started to dig.

It took weeks. At first it was black sand, then white sand, and at three to four metres deep, we were into clay. The well was lined with timber, with a basic ladder put in place. While my brothers and I took turns digging, Dad hoisted the sand and clay up to the surface, creating a great playground for those not down the well. We made roads and tunnels for our few rustic toy trucks that had been retrieved from the local rubbish tip!

At about six metres (20 feet) deep, water started to seep in, then a stronger flow another metre or so deeper. Each stream was different—one a little brackish, another slightly salty. There was the added challenge of keeping the water out while digging, lifting buckets of mud and water to the surface. But George and Steve had concluded that the best flow could be down further, just above rock—so we kept digging.

At eight metres (about 26 feet) deep, water flowed into the well and the water level rose quickly. Dad was joined by Mum as a bucket was brought to the surface. Both took long drinks from a big tin mug, looked at each other and concluded simply, "Hmm. Good water!"

We had dug deep. The streams had come together, and it was good water.

Streams of good water

A short while after offering the Samaritan woman living water—the "good Spirit" (Psalm 143:10, NIV)—at Jacob's well near Sychar, Jesus stopped by His boyhood hometown, Nazareth. Following His usual Sabbath practice, He went to the synagogue. Invited to read, He unrolled the Isaiah scroll, applying its messianic prophecies to Himself:

> The Spirit of the Lord is upon me, for he appointed me to bring Good News to the poor. He has sent me to proclaim that captives will be released, that the blind will see, that the oppressed will be set free, and that the time of the Lord's favour has come (Luke 4:18, 19; compare Isaiah 61:1, 2).

In Jesus, the Spirit's activities converged as *streams of living water*—flowing within and from Him. These have been identified as "great traditions of the Christian faith"—eternal truths that flowed from Jesus, and through the life of the early church:[1]

- *The incarnational stream.* Conceived by the Spirit, Jesus came into our world as "God with us" (Matthew 1:23, NIV). In doing mission work, we should be "with people" too.
- *The contemplative stream.* Like Jesus, we will be led by the Spirit to intentionally create times for prayer, to empower our daily service and disciple-making.
- *The inspirational stream.* Jesus the Living Word met the devil's temptations with the Spirit's inspired written Word, saying, "It is written" (Matthew 4:4, 6, 10, NIV).
- *The evangelism stream.* Jesus was "appointed" by the Spirit "to preach good news" (Luke 4:18). He commissioned His followers to do the same. We are to share the good news and the promise of the Spirit's presence (see Mark 16:9–16; Matthew 28:16–20; Acts 1:4–8).
- *The compassionate stream.* By His miracles, Jesus stood in the stream of social justice, with the poor, captives, blind, downtrodden and oppressed (see Luke 4:16–19). We are to show mercy, likewise.
- *The holiness stream.* Conceived by the Spirit, Jesus was "the holy one" (Luke 1:35, NIV), living a righteous life. By God's grace, His holiness is ours by faith.
- *The miraculous stream.* Full of the Spirit, Jesus' teaching was accompanied by miracles. He promised, "miraculous signs will accompany those who believe" (Mark 16:17)—and they did (see Acts 2:43).

Over the centuries, there were times when these streams or activities of the Spirit separated. We can see in history that when individual streams became the focus of the church, in isolation from the strength and witness of the other streams, these individual streams became excessive or toxic. This has resulted in the fragmentation of the church, weakening Christian witness.

Snakes and ladders—and good water

One morning as we peered down into our newly dug well, we saw movement. A deadly dugite snake—a species found only in Western Australia—had slipped into the well and was caught on a rung of the makeshift ladder two to three metres down. Dad lowered a bucket down, dislodged the snake and brought it to the surface. With some awe, we poked it with a branch and concluded in Australian boyish slang, "It's not a very happy chappy!"

All kids that grow up in the Australian bush know that snakes sun themselves and slither near water. And while the streams of the Spirit flowed fresh and clear in the life of Jesus and among His first followers, the distractions of evil were never far away. Unfortunately, zealots distorted the eternal truths of the Spirit's streams of activity. So don't be surprised if snakes turn up where there is *good* water.

The holiness stream has been muddied with legalism—external behaviours, works of righteousness, attempting by human will alone to live without sin.[2] But "all holiness is God's holiness in us."[3]

The compassionate stream is another that has been distorted. The early church struggled to accept that the gift of salvation and the Spirit's anointing for life and service were for all. Even today, churches remain divided over the equality and dignity afforded to all by the gospel. However, a sense of justice increasingly pervades secular society, and this might drag Christian churches to value people as the gospel dictates they should.

The miraculous stream is yet another that has suffered. Full of the Spirit, Jesus both taught the good news and performed miracles. He promised that "miraculous signs will accompany those who believe" (Mark 16:17). However, even in New Testament times, some in Corinth elevated the miraculous signs to being evidence of a superior spirituality. This was never Jesus' intent and Paul would have none of it (see 1 Corinthians 13:1; 14:18, 19).

We find identity in the activities of the Spirit

During and since the Reformation, many of the streams of the Spirit have been rediscovered, buried deep beneath the sands of human activity. And today, there is a renewed commitment to returning to the faith of Jesus and the Spirit. Following Jesus and His Spirit is increasingly defining missional movements, cultivating the apostles' vision of there being "no place left" where the gospel is not known (see Romans 15:14–24; compare Revelation 14:6–13).

As streams of water flow into one another, refreshing each other, so the streams of the Spirit complement one another. One is enriched by the others. Together, the streams form *rivers of living water*—good water—flowing from our hearts to invigorate, refresh, challenge and transform our homes, workplaces and communities.

Imagine mighty refreshing rivers, where all these streams of the Spirit flow together. I am not imagining ecumenism, but lives, homes, missional groups, local churches, mission agencies and even denominations where these converge in incarnational living and prayer, faithfulness to the Bible, gospel evangelism, compassion and justice, holiness and power.

These will be embracing rivers of missional engagement, deep rivers of divine intimacy and prayer, steady Word-centred rivers of inspiration and discernment, crystal clear rivers of God's amazing grace and salvation, broad rivers of unconditional love and justice for all people, and dancing powerful rivers of jubilation in holy living and the healing power of the Spirit.[4]

Where these rivers flow, there will be transformation and eternal life. And Jesus said, "Rivers of living water will flow from the heart of anyone who believes in me" (John 7:38, footnote).

EMPOWERED

Read Acts 19:1–20.

1. What streams of the Spirit converged to empower Paul's mission in Ephesus?

2. What happens when the streams of the Spirit are isolated from each other?
   - What excesses or aberrations do you observe?
   - When ministry and mission are institutionalised into silos or church departments, rather than embodied within missional groups, what is lost?

3. Jesus said, "Rivers of living water will flow from the heart of anyone who believes in me" (John 7:38, footnote).
   - How do you see these rivers flowing from your life?

- How could you bring the Spirit's activity to your family, workplace and community?

4. Review the streams of the Spirit that converge to form "rivers of living water." Which streams flow the strongest from your heart and life? What do they look like in practice?

CHAPTER 9

PRAYING FOR RAIN

Come, Holy Spirit, I need you,
Come Sweet Spirit, I pray,
Come in your strength and your power,
Come in your own gentle way.

Come, Holy Spirit, we need you,
Come Sweet Spirit, we pray,
Come in your strength and your power,
Come in your own gentle way.

Amen.[1]

With heads bowed, hundreds stood holding hands, quietly singing, "Come, Holy Spirit, I need you." The song was followed by a simple prayer thanking the Spirit that they could be part of His movement across their provinces and asking Him to direct their reading of Scripture, planning and witness. Then, in hushed tones, all prayed aloud in Pidgin and their local dialects.

We were in the Asaro district, the home of Papua New Guinea's famous mud-men. Movement leaders came in from the towns and villages of the mountainous Eastern Highlands and Chimbu regions. Businesspeople, professionals, farmers, and local church and mission leaders were following Jesus' simple, no-cost, anyone-can-do-it disciple-making methods. Weathered by their rugged environment and harsh social circumstances, their faces glowed with their love for Jesus Christ and the peace of the indwelling Spirit.

This was the third year in a row that hundreds had gathered across the provinces and in the nation's capital. For up to a week at a time, they came together to read of Jesus' disciple-making and movement-building methods in the gospels and the church-multiplication movement in the book of Acts. In each place, those participating sat in their district or provincial groups, working in teams of up to four, as they prayed and planned. All discussion of Scripture was based around the *Discovery Bible Reading* process (see Appendix A), so that each person participated in relating Jesus' life and methods to their places.

Now, thousands of *Discovery Bible Reading* groups are multiplying across the country—in village and city homes, businesses, workshops, government offices and on educational campuses—exploring the gospels and reading through books of the Bible.

Without display or babbling

In this movement, I have not witnessed repetitious prayers, shouting or babbling. The believers take Jesus' instruction seriously, and He said:

> When you pray, don't be like the hypocrites who love to pray publicly on street corners and in the synagogues where everyone can see them. . . . When you pray, don't babble on and on as the gentiles do. They think their prayers are answered merely by repeating their words again and again. Don't be like them, for your Father knows exactly what you need even before you ask him! (Matthew 6:5, 7, 8).

In some places, there is the regular practice of dawn prayer, with families or churches gathering before sunrise to sing quietly and pray. What they call *rain prayer* is also widely practiced, with all gathered praying aloud at the same time—but quietly, just above a whisper. Without display, shouting or repetitious ecstatic utterances, the believers earnestly pray in their own languages—Pidgin, local dialects and English. Communities are being saturated with the good news of Jesus' resurrection and the presence of His Spirit.

Hype versus assurance

If there is one Old Testament character with whom we associate the Holy Spirit, it is Elijah. Years of drought had reduced the land to a dust bowl. Even the king was out searching for feed for his cattle. Most felt that God's prophet was to blame—and, in a sense, he was![2]

Elijah called the Israelites and the priests of Baal and Asherah to a showdown on Mount Carmel. It was time for God's people to decide who they would follow—who they would depend on for rain. With the shimmering waters of the Mediterranean below, the 850 pagan prophets danced wildly around their altar, shouting, raving and slashing themselves, "but there was no reply of any kind"—and no rain (see 1 Kings 18:26–29).

At the time of the evening sacrifice, Elijah called the people together. He repaired the altar of the Lord, prepared wood for a fire and a bull for an offering, then he had barrels of water poured over the bullock, wood and altar stones. Elijah prayed to the living God to reveal that He was the God of Israel. His prayer was earnest and direct. Fire flashed from heaven—consuming the sacrifice and even the stones. The people cried, "The Lord—he is God! Yes, the Lord—he is God!" (1 Kings 18:39).

Then something remarkable happened. After three years of drought, a small cloud appeared over the sea. It rapidly moved toward them, "and soon the sky was black with clouds" (1 Kings 18:45). Rain began to fall. Torrential rain.

Effective prayer is not characterised by hype, dancing or repeated demands, but by the quiet assurance of a trusting authentic relationship with God.

Evil had been defeated—but Elijah ran. Both the rain and Jezebel pursued him until he was hundreds of kilometres south, hiding in a cave in the Sinai desert (see 1 Kings 19:1–9). There it seemed he was alone—but he was not.

He heard God ask:

> "What are you doing here, Elijah?" Elijah replied, "I have zealously served the Lord God Almighty. But the people of Israel have broken their covenant with you, torn down your altars, and killed every one of your prophets. I am the only one left, and now they are trying to kill me too" (1 Kings 19:9, 10).

Then, reminiscent of the time Moses came onto the same mountain to receive God's eternal commands, the Lord told Elijah, "'Go out and stand before me on the mountain.'. . . And as Elijah stood there, the Lord passed by" (1 Kings 19:11; compare Exodus 33:18–34:7).

First, a mighty windstorm hit—tearing rocks from the cliffs, "but the Lord was not in the wind" (1 Kings 19:11) Then a violent earthquake struck, followed by fire, but the Lord was not in them either. But "after the fire there was the sound of a gentle whisper. When Elijah heard it, he wrapped his face in his cloak and went out and stood at the entrance of the cave" (1 Kings 19:12, 13). The assuring presence of God's Spirit was found in quiet—after the turmoil of wind, earthquake and fire. God spoke in a whisper.

Praying for the Spirit

Jesus taught His disciples to pray—providing an example, illustrating trust in God and identifying what we should ask for (see Luke 11:1–13). Prayer is conversation with God—talking and listening. We can talk with Him any place, at any time, in groups and individually, walking or driving. We don't need to beat around the bush, but can talk simply, specifically and directly with Him.

When teaching how to pray, Jesus emphasised the priority of asking for the Holy Spirit:

> And so I tell you, keep on asking, and you will receive what you ask for. Keep on seeking, and you will find. Keep on knocking, and the door will be opened to you. For everyone who asks, receives. Everyone who seeks, finds. And to everyone who knocks, the door will be opened.
>
> You fathers—if your children ask for a fish, do you give them a snake instead? Or if they ask for an egg, do you give them a scorpion? Of course not! So if you sinful people know how to give good gifts to your children, how much more will your heavenly Father give the Holy Spirit to those who ask him (Luke 11:9–13).

What was He speaking of? What is the prayer that is always answered with a positive response? Jesus made it clear: praying for the Holy Spirit is to be our priority. It is His command. On the Thursday night before His crucifixion, He said:

> Yes, ask anything in my name, and I will do it. If you love me, obey my commandments. And I will ask the Father, and he will give you another Advocate, who will never leave you. He is the Holy Spirit, who leads into all truth (John 14:14–17; compare John 14:12–14).

Prayer for the Spirit's baptism is a *singular experience*, while praying for the Spirit's filling is a *daily privilege*. Spirit baptism is like Jesus' anointing at His baptism. It is not an extra second blessing for a select few but is God's anointing for the service and ministry to which we are all called. However, there is a fresh filling that we can experience daily.

Prayer for the Spirit's baptism is a singular experience, while praying for the Spirit's filling is a daily privilege.

Praying with the Spirit

Twice Paul wrote of "fellowship" or conversation with the Spirit (see 2 Corinthians 13:14; Philippians 2:1). He commanded the Ephesians to be "filled with the Holy Spirit" (Ephesians 5:18), urging them, "Pray in the Spirit at all times and on every occasion. Stay alert and be persistent in your prayers for all believers everywhere" (Ephesians 6:18; compare Jude 20). "Keep on praying" (1 Thessalonians 5:17), Paul encouraged the Thessalonians. "And continue to pray as you are directed by the Holy Spirit" (Jude 20).

We can have fellowship or conversation with the Spirit by praying through Scripture. The Spirit inspired Scripture, and when you read and reflect on it, you are engaging with His insights, directions and counsel. Read Bible books from beginning to end and experience His presence. Perhaps meet with friends once a week to read a Bible book, one story at a time, from beginning to end, using the *Discovery Bible Reading* method (see Appendix A).

It is also important to pray in community. We can enjoy the Spirit's presence in conversational prayer with others. This is also a great way for those who have never prayed to learn and to draw close to God—to pray in and with the Spirit (see Appendix B).

Prayer for the Spirit's filling is our daily opportunity. Just as Jesus came from times spent with the Father reinvigorated, so will we be refreshed and empowered by His filling.

EMPOWERED

Read Luke 11:1–13.

1. What have you discovered about praying *for* and *in* the Spirit?

2. What key ideas will you apply to your journey with the Spirit?

3. In what ways has your relationship with God been enriched by prayer songs or hymns?

4. How have you experienced the Spirit by kneeling before God and claiming the promise of Luke 11:9–13 for the Holy Spirit?

CHAPTER 10

BEING SPIRIT-FILLED DAILY

> After this prayer, the meeting place shook, and they were all filled with the Holy Spirit (Acts 4:31).

The promise of Holy Spirit baptism was fulfilled at Pentecost, with the outpouring of the Spirit and the birth of the Christian movement. As explained by Peter at that time, the gift of the Spirit (see Acts 1:4, 2:33, 38, 39)—which is the baptism or outpouring of the Spirit (Acts 1:5; 2:17, 33)—is as essential for our salvation as is the forgiveness of our sins.

The Spirit's baptism is one of the distinctive blessings for all who repent and believe—irrespective of gender, race, age or rank. All receive forgiveness and Spirit baptism (see Acts 2:17, 39). John Stott wrote that "far from being a dividing factor (some have it, others have not), [Spirit baptism] is the great unifying factor (an experience we have all had)."[1] This is our shared experience as Christians.

Both aspects of our conversion and salvation—the washing away of sin and the bestowal of the Holy Spirit—are linked in Spirit baptism. In our conversion by the Spirit, we are baptised or anointed by Him for life, witness and disciple-making. This is the "one baptism" (Ephesians 4:5) in water and Spirit that testifies to our faith and empowers us for service (see Matthew 28:16–20; Mark 16:9–17). And Paul insisted that "believers... receive the promised Holy Spirit through faith" (Galatians 3:14), not by any good works of obedience.

But are we growing with the Spirit? What is our ongoing experience with Him? While Paul affirmed that "we have all been baptised into one body by one Spirit" (1 Corinthians 12:13), he at the same time rebuked the Corinthian believers for being "infants in Christ" (1 Corinthians 3:1).

Daily Spirit-filling is needed

Why do we need to be filled with the Spirit each day?

First, it is important to understand what we mean when we say *filled*. On the day of Pentecost, the Spirit filled everyone He baptised. Spirit-filling was the *consequence* of Spirit baptism. We read that "everyone present was filled with the Holy Spirit" (Acts 2:4). As Robert W Lyon said, "From Pentecost on, all believers receive at conversion the Holy Spirit as promised—in His fullness. No biblical basis exists for a distinction between receiving the Spirit and being baptised in, or filled with, the Spirit."[2]

Spirit baptism always means Spirit-filling. However, while we do not read in the Bible of those who were baptised by the Spirit on Pentecost day being rebaptised by the Spirit, we do find those same believers being *filled* again. So, while Spirit baptism is the unique initiation associated with our conversion, Spirit-filling could be described as the ongoing, repeatable, deepening consequence of our conversion. Just as a 25-year-old athlete has a greater lung capacity than a newborn, so a mature Christian has a greater capacity for the Spirit than a newborn believer.[3] For this reason, while some have urged a daily baptism of the Spirit, I write of *daily filling*—keeping in mind Paul's command "to go on being filled [a continuous present imperative] with the Holy Spirit" (see Ephesians 5:18).[4]

According to the New Testament, we need to be filled with the Spirit daily:

1. Spirit-filling empowers us to live as Christians. God wants us to be full of the Spirit, like the seven chosen to serve in Jerusalem, Barnabas and newly converted disciples in Antioch in Pisidia (see Acts 6:3, 5; 11:24; 13:52).
2. Spirit-filling endows us with power for a particular ministry or mission. For example, John the Baptist (see Luke 1:15–17) and Saul (see Acts 9:17; compare 22:12–15; 26:16–23) were filled with the Spirit for their special ministries.
3. Spirit-filling equips us for an immediate task. The Spirit filled Zechariah and Elizabeth to equip them to prophesy and to have a son (see Luke 1:5–8, 41, 67), Peter, to equip him to meet the Sanhedrin (see Acts 4:8), the Jerusalem believers, to equip them to continue their witness in the face of opposition (see Acts 4:31), Stephen, to equip him to stand for his faith to the death (see Acts 7:55), and Paul, to equip him to rebuke the magician on Cyprus (see Acts 13:9).

Jesus was filled with the Spirit for all these three purposes: for living, mission and equipping for an immediate task (see Luke 3:22; 4:14, 18). He prayed for the Spirit's filling, and we are to as well.

When under threat from the same Jewish council that condemned Jesus to death, Peter and John found the other believers in Jerusalem and together they prayed:

> And now, O Lord, hear their threats, and give us, your servants, great boldness in preaching your word. Stretch out your hand with healing power; may miraculous signs and wonders be done through the name of your holy servant Jesus (Acts 4:29, 30).

They had been filled with the Spirit on the day of Pentecost (see Acts 2:4), and Peter was "filled with the Holy Spirit" (Acts 4:8) when standing before the religious council, yet the impact of further filling was immediate and dramatic: "The meeting place shook, and they were all filled with the Holy Spirit. Then they preached the word of God with boldness" (Acts 4:31).

The impact of further filling was immediate and dramatic.

Prayer for the Spirit's filling, refreshing, empowerment and miracles is a daily privilege. Just as Jesus came from times spent with the Father reinvigorated, so shall we.

How can we be filled with the Spirit?

We must invest quality time to develop a relationship with the Holy Spirit. Here are some practical steps for Spirit-filling that I have found really work:[5]

1. *Prayer*. Before starting the day, spend time with the Spirit and experience His fresh filling. It may take hours or even days of feeding on God's Word and longing for the Spirit's filling for our hunger and thirst to be quenched. Listen for His voice—for "his Spirit joins with our spirit to affirm that we are God's children" (Romans 8:16). He speaks through His Word. He provides encouragement and assurance. As we engage with colleagues, He provides insights into how to relate to and support one another. When "believers lifted their voices together in prayer...they were all filled with the Holy Spirit" (Acts 4:24, 31). Plan a regular weekly prayer time with friends or fellow believers. Gather and pray for the Spirit's filling.

2. *Bible reading*. Read the gospels, immersing yourself in the life and story of Jesus. Read the book of Acts—the activities of the Spirit in the body of Christ. It is inspiring and Spirit-filling. Read the New Testament letters as they were written—as letters. Most are short, so can easily be read from beginning to end. Try it. They are rich in encouragement about living in Christ or in the Spirit.
3. *Engage in mission*. While prayer and Bible reading are foundational, our prayers for Spirit-filling are not to be egocentric. Participation in His mission of disciple-making, church-planting and movement-building is an essential element for our Spirit-filling.

Before visiting neighbours, friends or family with opportunities to share the gospel, seek His wisdom and guidance. When we engage in sharing the gospel, multiplying disciples and cultivating missional communities, the Spirit is active. Trust the Spirit's presence and power (see Acts 1:4–8).

When we engage in mission, our prayers for life transformation—so that our speech, attitudes, submission, gratitude, worship, unity and generosity fully represent God—will be blended with prayers for courage or boldness to speak of Jesus to those in desperate need. This will bring His filling (see Acts 4:29–34).

What will it look like?

There will be different levels of maturity, but our families, friends and colleagues will see significant change in areas of our lives such as:

- *Speech*: we will start to be mindful of the impact of our words, and encourage each other in faithfulness and love (see Galatians 5:22–26).

- *Worship*: we will become concerned with honouring God (see Acts 2:38–47).
- *Attitude*: we will develop an attitude of thankfulness in and for all circumstances—in contrast to grumbling (see Ephesians 5:18–20).
- *Submission*: we will learn to humbly submit our will to God's will—"Not self-assertion but self-submission is the hallmark of the Spirit-filled Christian" (see Ephesians 5:21).[6]
- *Unity*: we will seek to put differences aside and work together with others for the sake of the mission of God (see Acts 4:32).
- *Generosity*: we will find joy in using our resources to care for others (see Acts 4:32–34).

The Spirit's presence is transformative, and Spirit-filling is on display for all to see. It is evident in our honour for God, our service to others, our gratitude, our attitude, in how we treat and speak to others—our family, friends, colleagues and even our pets—and in how we share the good news of salvation.

Some may mock us, as on Pentecost day, but in contrast to being unrestrained, irrational and out of control, those under the Spirit's influence will act like Jesus (see Ephesians 5:18–20).[7]

Some may mock us, as on Pentecost day, but in contrast to being unrestrained, irrational and out of control, those under the Spirit's influence will act like Jesus.

How can we be filled with the Spirit and know it?

Daily filling of the Spirit is our greatest need. This is our lack—and the lack in our churches. So how can we be filled? The solution is simple. Time for God—praying for Spirit rain and filling, reflecting on His Word, and participating in His mission.

How can we know if we are filled with the Spirit? Our families, friends and colleagues will see changes in our lives—in our speech, worship, attitudes, submission, unity and generosity as believers. We will also have courage and power in our witness to the saving and healing power of Jesus.

As rain in due season

We are as dependent on the Spirit as a farmer is dependent on rain in its due season. He waits for us to engage with Him. He seeks to reinvigorate us.

In one season of life, I was again reading through the Scriptures, enjoying the surprises of the Spirit's engagement with the patriarchs, prophets, kings and everyday people. I had read the stories of the Old Testament and was re-reading the gospels. Having attended a mission conference in Sydney, Australia, I had booked into a motel for the night before returning to my home in Melbourne.

In my reading, I had gotten to Luke 11. Reflecting on Jesus' teaching, I knelt with my Bible open at His promise in verses 9–13, simply saying, "Father, Jesus said that you will give the Holy Spirit to those who ask. I am asking. Thank you." I waited quietly, reflecting on God's goodness and grace. I did not repeat the name of Jesus, nor plead or cry out—but I was serious. And He came in warmth and light, filling me with peace.

That was a *fresh filling of the Spirit*—not my Spirit baptism.

Although Jesus has never appeared to me as He did to Paul in visions, I can relate to his experiences of the Spirit revealing Himself in tangible ways. In the midst of an extremely heavy schedule of evangelistic preaching, I arrived to share God's Word with a large congregation in Foksal Street, Warsaw, Poland. It was the practice in that church for the preacher to kneel quietly before preaching. I was exhausted and distinctly unwell, so it was not a time for meaningless repetition. I quietly asked for a fresh anointing of the Spirit, and He came. A physical sense of peace passed through me, and I stood refreshed without an ache or pain.

Again, that was a *fresh filling of the Spirit*—not my Spirit baptism.

I can also relate to the sense of being alone that Paul had on many occasions. The Spirit's presence and refreshing is not always evident or felt. There have been dark valleys of disappointment and despair, when there was no tangible response from God. But at all times—even during suffering, pain and tragedy—we can receive Him by faith and have the assurance that He walks with us and dwells in us (see Galatians 3:14; Romans 8:17–27).

We are dependent on Him

Sadly, we neglect the Spirit too often. We become complacent. We lapse into doing church and ministry with little more than a cursory nod toward Him. Our vision becomes jaded and our models, methods and evangelism packages irrelevant. Finely tuned systems, procedures, policies and sacraments leave little need for the Spirit's leading in the mission of the church, our strategising or decision-making. We even become careless about the devil's determination to distract and destroy.

The apocalyptic scriptures foretell chaotic end-times, with political powers disseminating fake news, faith systems devoid of biblical foundations, and superficial excitement posing as spirituality. But as unclean spirits and demons like frogs jump from the unholy trinity of evil—the dragon, beast and false prophet—we are promised that the earth will be brightened with the splendour of the gospel and refreshed with the final showers of the Spirit (see Revelation 16:12–15; 18:1–5).

Throughout history, deception, manipulation and human excitement have accompanied revivals, and these can be expected in the end times. But don't fear the true Spirit because of the false: "Do not stifle the Holy Spirit. Do not scoff at prophecies, but test everything that is said. Hold on to what is good" (1 Thessalonians 5:19–21).

We cannot live without the Spirit's presence and power for a moment. We are dependent on His counsel and empowerment in due season—at the right time.

Daily Spirit-filling is our greatest need. But God has promised to supply our lack—and *rivers of living water will flow from within.*

EMPOWERED

Read Acts 4:1–37.

1. Describe a time when you experienced a special filling of the Spirit:

2. Plan regular times to pray for the Holy Spirit's refreshing and filling:

   • What times might work best for you and what will be the focus of your prayer?

- As well as personal prayer, who could you invite to pray with you and when?

- How could a few days of spiritual retreat refresh you? When could you do this?

- What scripture will you reflect on?

- Who will you pray for each day?

3. In the light of the Spirit's filling, how do you understand the experiences of the Spirit speaking with and empowering early believers, as in Acts 13:1–4, 16:6–9 and 19:1–12?

4. Read accounts of prayer with "the laying on of hands" to affirm those serving God (see Acts 8:14–17, 9:17–19, 13:1–3, 19:1–7; compare Hebrews 6:1, 2).
   - Share the anointing of the Spirit. Who could you pray for and bless in this way, and when will you do this?

EMPOWERED: ENJOY HIS PRESENCE

Having grown up a short distance from the ocean, I enjoy the surf. I love the waves washing over me. Recently, after equipping local church leaders on Manus Island, Papua New Guinea, the hotel–airport shuttle took us around the coast. Through the trees, I could see the delight of small boys leaping from a high rock ledge into the deep Pacific waters.

Then, on my flight home to Australia, I found Kirsten Galliott, Editor-in-Chief of the Qantas in-flight magazine and a creative essayist, reflecting on the booming popularity of "retreats where wi-fi is limited (or non-existent)" with "opportunities for solitude and reflection." She wrote, "The world feels so noisy, so relentless. . . . The never-ending deadlines, the chock-a-block diaries, the urge to check our phones up to 80 times a day (or, according to one study, a shocking 150 times)."[1]

Galliott echoed the feelings of many when she wrote, "We just want to stop the noise." She described how she retreats from the overwhelming stress: she escapes to let time meander, enjoy a meal, walk in the open air, and do "a whole lot of swimming"—asking, "What is it about water that washes away the stress?"

It is invigorating and refreshing to feel the power of the sea, the rise and fall of the waves, and to be totally immersed. It's the same with living water.

Christ—at home in us

The Spirit refreshes, transforms and empowers. When Jesus announced His departure, He promised, "I will ask the Father, and he will give you another Advocate, who will never leave you" (John 14:16). It is not that the Spirit would be merely a substitute or stand-in, rather it would be a closer relationship: "He lives with you now and later will be in you" (John 14:17).

Jesus explained further:

> I will not abandon you as orphans—I will come to you. Soon the world will no longer see me, but you will see me. Since I live, you also will live. When I am raised to life again, you will know that I am in my Father, and you are in me, and I am in you. . . . [W]e will come and make our home with [you] (John 14:18-20, 23).

How real is this? Is it simply a poetic way of expressing a lofty sentiment? Or can we take it to mean what it says: that by the Holy Spirit, Christ actually lives in us and makes His home in our lives?

Paul experienced it as a reality, describing the "inner strength" that God gives "through his Spirit," adding: "Then Christ will make his home in your hearts as you trust in him" (Ephesians 3:16, 17).

The Spirit brings the presence of God into our lives. Through His filling and indwelling presence, the early disciples were closer to Jesus than when He walked the dusty roads with them. One of my seminary teachers called this the biblical doctrine "of the Real Presence," quoting the little book *Steps to Christ*: "But even here Christians may have the joy of communion with Christ; they may have the light of His love, the perpetual comfort of His presence."[2] Ellen White also wrote of the disciples, "The light, and love, and power of the indwelling Christ shone out through them, so that [others], beholding, 'marvelled . . . that they had been with Jesus.'"[3] Where is Jesus? He is at "home" in us. This is ours to enjoy.

Enjoy life in the Spirit

In many Bibles, the heading given to Romans 8 is "Life in the Spirit." Making the point that "there is no condemnation for those who belong to Christ Jesus" (Romans 8:1), Paul underscores that "the power of the life-giving Spirit has freed you from the power of sin that leads to death" (Romans 8:2). We don't have to carry the past—we are free of condemnation and we enjoy new life.

The Spirit gives new thoughts (see Romans 8:5) and new life (see Romans 8:6–11). Paul wrote that "letting the Spirit control your mind leads to life and peace" (Romans 8:6). We are also adopted into His family (see Romans 8:15). Think about this and the end-time implications: "The Spirit of God, who raised Jesus from the dead, lives in you. And just as God raised Christ Jesus from the dead, he will give life to your mortal bodies by this same Spirit living within you" (Romans 8:11).

He leads and empowers us to live as "children of God" (Romans 8:14), and "testifies with our spirit that we are God's children" (Romans 8:16, NIV). This does not mean we are super-Christians, but "we think about things that please the Spirit" (Romans 8:5; compare Romans 8:12). While our natures are sinful, He lives in us, leading and drawing us away from lives of sin (see Romans 8:12–16).

Walk the dark valleys with the Spirit

The unfair way in which suffering and death choose their innocent victims can really rattle and challenge faith—global and personal tragedies, road accidents and trauma, viruses and cancer, abuse and domestic violence. Millions struggle amid poverty and oppression, lives are devastated by war and disease, the innocent suffer. I cannot accept that such tragedies reflect God's sovereign will or represent some twisted plan to mature the faith of His children.

Writing of life in the Spirit, Paul did not gloss over tragedy. He described a groaning creation, groaning believers, and a groaning Spirit. We don't need to be environmental activists to see that we are destroying our planet. The way we are living is not sustainable. Some might disagree about climate change and global warming, but the future of our planet can seem grim. Paul observed, "all creation has been groaning…right up to the present time" (Romans 8:22).

Believers do not escape the trauma of this world: "And we believers also groan, even though we have the Holy Spirit within us…for we long for our bodies to be released from sin and suffering" (Romans 8:23; compare 2 Corinthians 5:4).

Where is the Spirit as we go through deep valleys of suffering, tragedy and death? Paul declares, "we have the Holy Spirit within us.…And the Holy Spirit helps us in our distress" (Romans 8:23, 26). He adds:

> For example, we don't know what God wants us to pray for. But the Holy Spirit prays for us with groanings that cannot be expressed in words. And the Father who knows all hearts knows what the Spirit is saying, for the Spirit pleads for us believers in harmony with God's own will (Romans 8:26, 27).

In our darkest valleys, the Spirit groans with us. He is living within us as we struggle through painful tragic experiences, in the midst of this groaning world. He never leaves us but joins Jesus in interceding for us (see Romans 8:27, 34, NIV). Nothing can separate us from Him (see Romans 8:29–39).

Enjoy the fruit

The Holy Spirit is now "the Spirit of God living in you" (Romans 8:9). By virtue of Jesus' ministry in the world, the Spirit received a new identity—testifying of Jesus and bringing glory to Him (see John 15:26; 16:12–15). When He lives in us, He produces delightful fruit in our lives: "love, joy, peace, patience, kindness, goodness, faithfulness, gentleness and self-control" (Galatians 5:22, 23). Paul said, "let the Holy Spirit fill and control you … sing psalms and hymns and spiritual songs" (Ephesians 5:18-20). This is good, sweet fruit.

We see it in the early believers. They shared with great joy and generosity (see Acts 2:42–47), and with courage, unity, compassion and powerful witnessing (see Acts 4:31–35). Relax and enjoy this fruit in your own life.

Enjoy His baptism

Calvary and Pentecost are forever and inextricably linked. At Calvary, the intimacy of the Father, Son and Holy Spirit was dramatically displayed. On the Friday, this relationship was fractured—the Father from the Son and the Son from His Spirit (see Matthew 27:45–50). But, on resurrection Sunday morning, imagine the celebrations when Jesus was "raised to life in the Spirit" (1 Peter 3:18) "by the glorious power of the Father" (Romans 6:4; compare John 2:19).

That evening Jesus breathed on His disciples saying, "Receive the Holy Spirit" (John 20:22).[4] It was an anointing like Jesus received at His baptism. As we have seen, this promise was realised at Pentecost and we also receive the same with our "one baptism" (Ephesians 4:5) in water and the Spirit.

On the day of Pentecost, Peter declared, "God has raised this Jesus to life, and we are all witnesses of it. Exalted to the right hand of God, he has received from the Father the promised Holy Spirit and has poured out what you now see and hear" (Acts 2:32, 33, NIV). Since then we have lived in the era of the Spirit's baptism, when "the Holy Spirit is giving life" (2 Corinthians 3:8).

The Spirit makes us alive spiritually, convicting and converting us. Our baptism in water and Spirit testifies to new life in Jesus and anointing to service and disciple-making. From the beginning to the end of our salvation and Christian growth, the Spirit works in us. There is no need for a second blessing, for He continually lives in us. In this way, Spirit baptism:

- *Creates a new dynamic for living—a new inner power.* "This means that anyone who belongs to Christ has become a new person. The old life is gone; a new life has begun!" (2 Corinthians 5:17).

- *Binds us to Jesus with unbreakable ties.* Jesus continues to be present in this world in the lives of His followers. Paul reflected on this reality: "It is no longer I who live, but Christ lives in me. So I live in this earthly body by trusting in the Son of God, who loved me and gave himself for me" (Galatians 2:20).

- *Creates a new community—the body of Christ.* As we lurched over the rocky road to the Rumba Mission on Bougainville, the building-projects manager Aaron Darius told me, "Mum died early of cancer, my sister was killed in an accident on her return home from sharing a health presentation, and my dad died a few years ago. I now just have a younger brother, my wife and child—and I have the church. When you have the fellowship of God's people, you still have family" (see Acts 2:42–47).

- *Anoints us for disciple-making.* Jesus was baptised in the Jordan and, at the same time, anointed by the Spirit for His ministry (see Luke 3:21, 22). Likewise, on Pentecost day, when the first believers were anointed by the Spirit, the Christian movement was born (see Acts 1:8). And

Peter declared that with *repentance* and *baptism* the promises of *forgiveness* and *the Spirit* are for all—"to you and to your children, and even to the Gentiles," he said to the crowds in the street, "all who have been called by the Lord our God" (Acts 2:38, 39).

- *Empowers our witness.* As with the apostles, our service, witness and ministry are the Spirit's activities. Many were converted in New Testament times by the gospel of Jesus Christ, with miracles attracting attention and relieving suffering—and this is still God's plan today (see Mark 16:15–18).[5]

These works of the Spirit are not for stage shows, attracting attention to performance faith-healers. During my internship for ministry, I learned the simplicity and power of anointing prayer from my mentor Pastor Bill Otto. At times, we were called to homes by those suffering ill-health or enslaved to addictions; at other times, we met them while out visiting. Inquiring about their faith, Bill simply explained the provision of prayer and anointing and then we prayed, placing a small amount of oil on the forehead of the person as a symbol of the Spirit's presence and power. There was no shouting, demanding or display. That is not necessary. The Spirit answers "the prayer offered in faith" (James 5:15, 16)—not always with physical healing or even mental health, but always with peace and assurance.

With the Spirit's baptism and filling, "rivers of living water will flow from the heart of anyone who believes" (John 7:38, footnote). Streams of grace and salvation, incarnational mission and witnessing, divine intimacy and prayer, Word-centred counsel and discernment, unconditional love and unwavering justice, righteousness and healing compassion will flow from us to bless and enrich our families, colleagues, friends and neighbours.

Enjoy His filling

Rejoice that the Spirit fosters good—morality, honesty, kindness, justice, obedience, respect and love within families. And rejoice that the Spirit restrains evil. You cannot expect accolades from this world, for its values are at variance to yours. Jesus said, "the world hates you"—it seeks to diminish, destroy and devour (see John 15:18–25). However, the Spirit curbs this outrage of malice; Satan's nefarious activities would be many times worse if not for the Spirit's restraining presence.

So enjoy living in the Spirit, or in Christ, and be constantly overawed with the reality that He brings the eternal Triune God to live within you.

Catching the waves of the Spirit

Actively look for the moving of the Spirit around you, then identify with that activity. Like a surfer looking for the waves of God's doing, see where the Spirit is working to build waves around us.[6]

We cannot make the waves. Only the Spirit can cultivate spiritual receptivity and then create waves of conviction, conversion, spiritual growth and revival. But we can learn where the waves are most likely found—often in the community, rather than in large churches—and join Him on the waves.

We cannot make the waves. . . . But we can learn where the waves are most likely found . . . and join Him on the waves.

Catching the waves looks easy. It is fun, but it takes faith, insight, skill, patience and—most of all—balance (see Luke 10:1–24). Just as we cannot manufacture ocean waves, our gimmicks, glossy programs and marketing techniques are ineffective in forming the waves of the Spirit. And in Jesus' life, teachings and commission, we find the only effective way to catch these waves. Jesus' methods are free—except for time and sacrificial love—and anyone can follow them.

In *If You Can Eat, You Can Make Disciples*, I wrote of cooperating with the Spirit in a way "that is not aggressively oppositional, blandly compromising nor merely graciously accommodating . . . an approach to sharing that is not tainted with pride, superiority and exclusivity—and that guards against such attitudes."[7] Cooperating with the Spirit "could be called a *conversational* or an *experiential* approach, and it is—but let us not lose the simplicity and strength of this approach in words." I therefore "simply define this alternative as *eating their food*!"[8]

Following Jesus' example and teaching, cooperating with the Spirit is relational: eat with people—listening to their stories; support, encourage and heal—sharing your story; and tell God's story—introducing the gospel and the assurance of His Spirit's presence (see Luke 10:8, 9).

We are experiencing an unprecedented movement of God's Spirit in many parts of our world. The Spirit is creating wave after wave of people receptive to the gospel. There are opportunities wherever believers are prepared and willing to engage. Christ's method of disciple-making and movement-building will be effective.[9]

Many are thirsty!

Ours is an increasingly bizarre world. World leaders label truth as fake, mainline news is manipulated by financial interests, public opinion is swayed by social media trolls, popular spirituality lacks biblical foundations and many fear the growing risks of human extinction. But, while chaotic, we live in the most opportune times for the Spirit.

Many are thirsty. Some are lonely, isolated, despairing, depressed, struggling and fearful. Others are busy in a round of activity, unaware of what or who could quench their nagging brokenness and thirst. Jesus is the well of salvation, the Spirit is the living water. *Rivers* of life-giving water are ours for the asking—for ourselves, then flowing through us to others (see John 7:38; compare 1 Corinthians 3:16, 17; 6:19, 20).

Holy Spirit baptism and His daily filling are ours to appreciate and enjoy. But more than that, we are totally dependent on Him. He makes us alive spiritually, draws us to Jesus and converts us. We are thoroughly changed by Him.

When "the Spirit of the Lord" came upon King Saul, he was "changed into a different person" (1 Samuel 10:6). When baptised by the Spirit on the day of Pentecost, the early believers became different people—faithful and fearless. And we experience the same.

Spirit baptism transforms us. It is not optional. And, as with the early believers, the Spirit's daily filling also transforms our lives and witness.

Without Him, our souls are thirsty, our churches are powerless, our denominations are lifeless, and our children, youth, families and communities see little relevance in our faith. The Spirit longs for our attention, trust and fellowship. He who has baptised us wants to fill us daily.

What are we waiting for? The Holy Spirit's daily filling is our greatest and most desperate need. As repeated again and again in the New Testament epistles and in this book, the solution is simple. Time with God—praying for rain and filling. Then He comes and we experience His powerful presence.

If we are thirsty, we can be Spirit-filled—refreshed and empowered daily—and rivers of living water will flow out from within—enriching, blessing and saving our families, friends and neighbours. So let us allow "God's generosity" to flow through us and "God will be given glory in everything through Jesus Christ. All glory and power belong to him forever and ever. Amen" (1 Peter 4:10, 11).

EMPOWERED

Read Romans 15:14–24.

1. Paul wrote his missionary letter to believers in Rome in the winter of AD 56–57. What two historic realities motivated his life and witness? How is your life constantly defined by these? See Romans 15:15–16.

2. How do you understand Paul's vision of sharing Christ where He was not known—with "no more place" (NIV) where he needed to share the gospel? See Romans 15:20, 23.

3. What sense of security and assurance is experienced by those living in the Spirit, even though our sinful nature is with us until Jesus comes? See Romans 8:1–16.

4. What does it mean to share life in the Spirit in the midst of chaos, suffering and pain, with both the Spirit and Jesus "interceding for us"? See Romans 8:17–27.

5. Where do you see the influence of the Holy Spirit in the lives of family members, among friends and work colleagues, or in your community? How could you engage with that activity and be the source of a river of living water?

APPENDIX A

DISCOVERY BIBLE READING

Invite two or three friends, family or colleagues to join you and share some food and drink together.

Each person should get or download an easy-to-read Bible translation.

Choose a Bible book to read together. The Gospel of Mark (only 20 pages) is a great place to start.

Without religious language, one could pray or read this prayer:

> *Dear God, please guide us. Thank you. Amen.*

Read one story or section per session. Have one person read the whole story, then another person read it again. Finally, have another person tell the story in their own words.

After reading, discuss the story using these five questions:

- What is new?
- What surprises you?
- What don't you understand?
- What will we apply or obey?
- What will we share this week with another?

If you have divergent ideas or unanswered questions that is OK. Just keep reading.

End by praying this prayer for each other, with your eyes open:

> *Dear God, thank you for your Word. Help us to follow you. Amen.*

Plan to meet and share again to explore the next story. Invite others to join you and encourage others to form groups.

When you meet to read again, you could ask:

- Who have you met or caught up with?
- What two things did you learn about those you met?
- How did we go applying the insights from last time?
- How did we go sharing?

When you finish reading Mark, Acts is a great next book.

APPENDIX B

CONVERSATIONAL PRAYER

Conversational prayer is a relaxed and enjoyable experience of prayer, even for those who are hesitant or inexperienced in praying. It is a natural and easy way to pray in groups—in cafes, at home, at the office or outdoors.

It is talking with friends and including God:

- It does not move around the circle.
- It is not a series of disconnected speeches.
- It explores a range of themes and issues.
- No-one dominates—some share more, others enjoy listening.
- All are actively listening and participating—no-one focuses on what they will say next.
- There is quiet reflection, discussion, laughter, support and encouragement.

Ideas and suggestions for conversational prayer with God and friends:

1. With God, discuss one subject at a time, for example: praise, thanks, issues or requests.

2. There is no need to list prayer requests. Let these arise naturally in conversation.
3. Listen to others as they pray, then affirm and respond to their prayers.
4. Each person can pray briefly and often or remain silent to enjoy the conversation.
5. Clarify the prayers of others, so you can pray intelligently.
6. Keep your eyes open to see and affirm those who are praying.
7. Avoid religious language. Speak naturally and directly.
8. Don't pray around the circle and avoid putting pressure on people.
9. Enjoy silence—enjoy being with friends and God.

Don't make prayer complicated. Prayer is talking with God, so simply expand your conversations to include Him.

APPENDIX C

SECOND BLESSING: THE MERGING OF PERFECTIONISM AND GLOSSOLALIA

By the end of the 19th century, streams of the Spirit long separated by the falling away of the Christian faith were again drawing life from each other. Lost truths were being rediscovered, and the long Dark Ages of Medieval church history were receding.

However, as the promises of Christ's return were rediscovered, the urgent preparations to be ready produced a quest for holiness and the Spirit that reached fever pitch. This gave rise to a type of *perfectionism*, the idea of living without sin at a level of holiness superior to that of the apostles, as well as the concept of a *second blessing*, with dramatic spiritual gifts considered to be evidence of this end-time righteousness.

This is a brief overview of the merging of these two ideas.

A superior level of holiness

Montanus (2nd century AD) first popularised the idea that believers can be more righteous than the apostles. Together with the Pelagian heresy (4th century AD) that sin taints rather than devastates, the stage was set for the concept of an end-time or last-generation righteousness or power over sin.

John Wesley, the founder of Methodism, revived this idea of Christian perfection, developing his doctrine of *entire sanctification.*[1] From the premise that involuntary errors arising from ignorance are not sin, he outlined three stages. First, a new Christian might voluntarily sin, needing confession; later, there would be victory over temptation and evil thoughts; and finally, the mature Christian would reach entire sanctification and not commit sin.[2]

The 19th century saw a revival of this emphasis on Christian perfection or holiness within American Methodism. Phoebe Palmer, a pioneer of the holiness movement, promoted a "shorter way" to entire sanctification through "altar theology." She saw sanctification as "an instantaneous act accomplished through the exercise of faith,"[3] where all worldly desires were sacrificed on the altar. Rather than relying on God's grace in the Spirit's quickening, saving and sanctifying power alone, the one work of the Spirit for salvation (justification) and Christian growth (sanctification) was separated—with entire sanctification possible instantly.

The urgent need to be ready for Jesus' soon return generated numerous end-times charts. Some separated the Spirit's ongoing work—that is, from Jesus' ascension to second coming—into two seasons: the autumn (early) rain following Pentecost and a last-day spring (latter) rain, with a gap of centuries between. It was suggested that a higher level of holiness than that of the apostles would be required before Jesus came back, with only those living without sin ready to meet Him (as illustrated).

Salvation
by faith in Jesus
plus our obedience

Superior level of living
without known sin by God's grace
plus our righteous works

At the end of time
only those living without sin
will be ready to meet Jesus

An illustration of the beliefs of the holiness movement—distorted by perfectionism.

The Wesleyan Pentecostal movement represented by Palmer emphasised a three-part pattern of blessing: first, the work of grace for conversion or new birth; second, the cleansing of the heart in entire sanctification; and finally, the baptism of the Holy Spirit.[4]

Their search for the evidence of Spirit baptism led to a focus on dramatic miracles and speaking in tongues. Some found support for an initial experience of faith and a later second blessing, and for separating justification (a work of faith) from sanctification (which they thought of as a superior righteousness), within the frames of dispensationalism—the idea that God saves in different ways in different eras.[5]

In the 1890s, a holiness movement from Keswick, in England's Lakes District, had significant influence in Adventism through Alonzo Jones—editor of the *Review and Herald* periodical. He "created a great charismatic revival in Adventism," fostering a "perfectionist and charismatic theology" quite different to his earlier 1888 righteousness-by-faith teaching.[6] However, testing the manifestations by the Word—including the aberrant idea of *holy flesh*—the idea of an end-time holiness superior to that of the apostles, along with dramatic miracles and glossolalia being the special evidences of a *second blessing* and Spirit baptism were rejected by Seventh-day Adventists.[7]

A superior spiritual gift

The biblical evidence is clear that all Christians are Spirit-baptised as an essential aspect of our conversion experience. While there is no scriptural basis for dividing the "one baptism" (Ephesians 4:5) of water and Spirit, none for a second level of perfectionism, and no suggestion that speaking in tongues is a superior gift that all believers must receive as evidence of Spirit baptism—in fact, Paul taught the opposite!—these became the foundations of the modern tongues movement.

William Seymour, the African-American who pioneered the 1906 Los Angeles "Azusa Street Revival," spent years immersed in holiness-perfectionism—especially its emphasis on charismatic manifestations. The Azusa Street Revival began as a revolutionary social movement, with the integration of marginalised people, the participation of women in spiritual leadership, including anointing prayer, and the idea that the gospel removed all status barriers. Seymour suffered swift and sustained opposition for these ideas. But his ideas about Spirit baptism gained acceptance and have become widespread. While like Wesley and Palmer, he saw "divine love" as "the central reality of the Spirit's presence," he claimed tongues to be "one of the signs that go with every baptised person."[8] Azusa Street is associated with the birth of modern Pentecostalism, with dramatic miracles and glossolalia being seen as the evidence of Spirit baptism.[9]

As illustrated on the next page, the two phases of holiness-perfectionism provided the setting for this emphasis on glossolalia or ecstatic tongues-speaking as the evidence of a second blessing.

The quest for holiness and evidence merged

The pursuit of evidence for a second blessing shifted the focus from the Spirit and His message to dramatic manifestations. People became preoccupied with seeking miracles and tongues-

Salvation by faith in Jesus plus our obedience	**Superior level of living** without known sin by God's grace plus our righteous works

Two phases of holiness perfectionism

Second blessing of Pentecostalism

Baptism by water	**Baptism by the Spirit** Second blessing—the charisma of the Spirit, ecstatic tongues-speaking

The two-phases of holiness perfectionism and the second blessing of Pentecostalism.

speaking as evidence of their salvation, with the risk of sidelining or neglecting the Spirit. Emotional revivalist preaching, intense music, shouting and crying out resulted in people being "slain in the Spirit" or falling down, accompanied by speaking in tongues. These experiences were considered evidence of a superior level of holiness.

There have been three waves of Pentecostalism, with some hoping for a fourth. The first wave, around 1900, was when Pentecostal churches began and speaking in tongues was considered synonymous with Spirit baptism. The second wave of Pentecostalism (neo-Pentecostalism) began in the 1960s, with speaking in tongues entering other churches—Catholic and Protestant. The third wave developed in the 1980s, with its emphasis on power evangelism and renewal worship; it was heavily dependent on repeated choruses and electronic amplification.[10]

While David Pawson, an evangelical-charismatic, acknowledged that a second blessing is without grounding in Scripture, dividing what is inherently connected in the "one baptism," he envisioned a fourth wave of Pentecostalism, where charismatics and evangelicals will come together in pragmatic, contagious and personal enthusiasm for the reconciliation of the streams of the Spirit.[11]

Experience vs the Word

As modernism gave way to postmodernism, objectivity to subjectivity, and evidence to experience, the Word was supplanted by manifestations—and the modern-day tongues-speaking movement rose in popularity.

Where does this leave us? According to the New Testament, Spirit baptism takes place as part of conversion and salvation, not later—and, whether living in the first or 21st centuries, all are saved only by the grace of the Father, the love of Jesus, and the justifying and sanctifying work of the Holy Spirit (as illustrated below).

There are no biblical foundations for:

- A superior end-time righteousness: a level of holiness greater than the apostles.
- Dividing baptism into two phases: salvation and a second blessing.
- Spirit baptism taking us to a superior spiritual realm.
- Dramatic gifts of miracles and tongues being seen as the evidence of Spirit baptism.

Conviction, conversion and baptims by the Spirit

One baptism–water & Spirit
Spirit baptism
- **A singular experience**
- **Anointed into the body of Christ**

Spirit-filling–a fresh daily experience

The work of the Spirit–all holiness is God's holiness:
- **by faith in Jesus–we are holy (justification)**
- **by faith in Jesus–we live and grow as Christians (sanctification)**

An illustration of the Biblical teaching of Spirit baptism and righteousness by faith.

On the day of Pentecost, Peter explained that repentance and baptism into Jesus' name bring the two promised blessings of the new covenant—forgiveness and Spirit baptism (see Acts 2:38, 39). These blessings are for all and are not to be separated—but they do not mean that we are sinless, nor engaged in exceptional, supernatural acts all the time. Paul made it clear that if you haven't received the Spirit you are not a Christian (see Romans 8:15) and that all believers are baptised in the Spirit—including those who do not speak in tongues (see 1 Corinthians 12:12, 13).

These are some of my greatest concerns:

- Without the corrections of all streams of the Spirit, perfectionism and glossolalia have merged to form the most popular spiritual force today.
- In separating Calvary (the gospel) from Pentecost (the Spirit), and inspiration (the Word) from the miraculous (the charismatic), we are left in a strange place.
- We have a popular spirituality without the objective foundation of the written Word (the Bible) or living Word (Jesus).

In a time of great shame, David cried out, "Do not cast me from your presence or take your Holy Spirit from me" (Psalm 51:11, NIV). And our prayers today must call for believers to experience rivers of living water, with the faithful convergence of all streams of the Spirit—not just one or two.

NOTES

Water: A Priority

1. “Thirst trap,” Dictionary.com, <https://www.dictionary.com/e/slang/thirst-trap>.
2. C Chocano, “It’s Easy to Be Called ‘Thirsty’ on Social Media,” *The New York Times Magazine*, April 4, 2017, <https://www.nytimes.com/2017/04/04/magazine/its-easy-to-be-called-thirsty-on-social-media-what-about-on-capitol-hill.html>.
3. ibid.

Chapter 1 If You Are Thirsty

1. For a description, see M Posner, “The Joyous Water-Drawing Ceremony,” <www.chabad.org/library/article_cdo/aid/1971019/jewish/The-Joyous-Water-Drawing-Ceremony.htm>.
2. See Revelation 22:1, 2; Zechariah 14:8, 9; compare Revelation 21:6–8.

Chapter 2 Living Water

1. D F Stramara, “Gregory of Nyssa’s Terminology for Trinitarian Perichoresis,” *Vigiliae Christianae*, Vol 52, No 3 (August, 1998), pages 257–263, < www.jstor.org/stable/1584502>.
2. J J Parsons, “Hebrew Names for God,” *Hebrew for Christians*, <www.hebrew4christians.com/Names_of_G-d/Spirit_of_God/spirit_of_god.html>.
3. E H Bickersteth (1969), *The Trinity*, Kregel, page 128. Bickersteth writes of the word *eternal*: “This is the same word which is used of the self existence from everlasting to everlasting of Jehovah.”
4. *The Holy Bible, New International Version* (1986), “Preface,” Holman Publishers, page ix.
5. Bickersteth, op cit, page 120.
6. J Oswald Sanders (1940), *The Holy Spirit and His Gifts*, Marshall, Morgan & Scott, page 24.
7. T Armitage (1890), *A History of the Baptists*, Bryan, Taylor & Co, page 39. Marcion was told this by Augustine.
8. The term *Godhead* is used three times in the *King James Version*: Acts 17:29, Romans 1:20 and Colossians 2:9.

Chapter 4 What is Holy Spirit Baptism?

1. A A Hoekema (1972), *Holy Spirit Baptism*, Eerdmans Publishing, pages 17–18. The preposition *in* is used in the seven instances of "to be baptised *in* the Holy Spirit": four in the Gospels, twice in Acts, and once in 1 Corinthians.
2. Some have wondered whether John the Baptist's diet might have been the carob bean, also called locust. But while the carob tree flourishes in the Judean hills and on the slopes of Galilee, it does not grow in the desert heat of the Dead Sea valley.
3. J R W Stott (1975), *Baptism and Fullness: The Work of the Holy Spirit Today*, Inter-Varsity, page 23. Stott calls John the Baptist "the last prophet of the old order."
4. ibid, page 24.
5. Through Jeremiah, God promised, "I will make a new covenant. . . . I will put my instructions deep within them, and I will write them on their hearts. . . . I will forgive their wickedness, and I will never again remember their sins" (Jeremiah 31:31–35). And through Ezekiel, "I will sprinkle clean water on you, and you will be clean. . . . I will put my Spirit in you" (Ezekiel 36:25, 27).
6. Stott, op cit, page 22.
7. ibid, page 23.
8. R G Gromacki (1972), *The Modern Tongues Movement*, Presbyterian and Reformed Publishing, page 60.
9. K Kuas, Volunteers in Action Coordinator, Madang Manus, Papua New Guinea, personal conversation at a Cultivating Movements Conference, Madang, January 27–29, 2020.
10. See Gromacki, op cit, pages 69–79 and G F Hasel (1991), *Speaking in Tongues: Biblical Speaking in Tongues and Contemporary Glossolalia*, ATS Publications, page 58, endnotes, for a discussion of the authenticity and incongruities of the so-called "longer ending" of Mark (Mark 16:9–20).
11. In Galatians 3:26–28 and Ephesians 4:4, 5, Paul also stressed that baptism secures unity in the one body of all believers regardless of national, social or sexual distinctions. And there is ground to believe that Romans 6:3, 4 and Colossians 2:12 are primarily pointing to Holy Spirit baptism.
12. Hoekema, op cit, page 17.

Chapter 5 Surprised by the Spirit

1. R R Hegstad (1974), *Rattling the Gates*, Review and Herald.
2. P Roennfeldt (2019), *Following the Apostles' Vision*, Signs Publishing, pages 15–24, for more on the tipping point of mission.

3. L R Froom (1956), *The Coming of the Comforter*, Review and Herald, page 142. Froom writes, “Paul was not asking concerning the special gifts of the Spirit, but of the Gift supreme—the Holy Spirit Himself... He wanted to learn whether they had received the filling of the Holy Spirit—the permanent, central feature of Pentecost. For there is an experience beyond the initial step by which the Holy Spirit first reveals sin, and begets a new life in the soul, and that is to be filled with the Spirit. For lack of this, one's testimony is feeble and the spiritual life but partial.”
4. The words *ordained* and *ordination* are not New Testament or biblical terms and have loaded meanings, so are not used.
5. R G Gromacki (1972), *The Modern Tongues Movement*, Presbyterian and Reformed Publishing, pages 56–59.
6. A A Hoekema (1972), *Holy Spirit Baptism*, William B Eerdmans Publishing, page 21.

Chapter 6 Rain

1. R Rice, “Rediscovering the Spirit-filled Life,” <www.sdanet.org/atissue/new/spiritualdiscernment/spiritlife.html>.
2. For more, see P Roennfeldt (2019), *Following the Apostles' Vision*, Signs Publishing, pages 87–88.
3. M Frost and A Hirsch (2003), *The Shaping of Things to Come*, Hendrickson, page 225.
4. Rice, op cit.

Chapter 7 Autumn and Spring Rain

1. See G Smeaton (1974), “Historical survey of the doctrine of the Holy Spirit,” *The Doctrine of the Holy Spirit* (reprint of 1889 edition), Banner of Truth Trust, pages 291–414, for a survey of the doctrine of the Holy Spirit from the Apostolic Period to the late 19th century.
2. ibid, page 296.
3. ibid, pages 300–303.
4. ibid, pages 303–307.
5. ibid, pages 309, 312, 319–322. The arbitrary, unauthorised way in which this truth of the Spirit was inserted as the *filioque* into the Nicene-Constantinopolitan creed by the Western Church at the Council of Toledo (589 AD) further fuelled acrimonious debate and the schism between East and West in 1054.
6. ibid, page 365.

7. A L White (editor), *Charismatic Experiences in Early Seventh-day Adventist History*, Ellen G White Estate. This is a reprint of 12 articles published in the *Review and Herald*, from August 10, 17, 24, 1972; March 15, 22, 29, April 5, 12, 19, 26, and August 2, 9, 1973.
8. White, op cit, page 12.
9. Smeaton, op cit, page 332.
10. ibid, page 337, quoting Augustine's testimony.
11. R Rice, "Rediscovering the Spirit-filled Life," <www.sdanet.org/atissue/new/spiritualdiscernment/spiritlife.html>.

Chapter 8 Rivers Flowing from Within

1. R J Foster (1998), *Streams of Living Water: Celebrating the Great Traditions of the Christian Faith*, HarperCollins, page xvi. Foster explores six of these: (1) contemplative, (2) holiness, (3) charismatic, (4) social justice, (5) evangelical and (6) incarnational.
2. ibid, pages 91–94.
3. ibid, pages 95–96.
4. ibid, page xv, for the inspiration for this summary.

Chapter 9 Praying for Rain

1. "Come, Holy Spirit, I Need You" by William J Gaither © 1964 William J. Gaither, Inc. (Admin by SHOUT! Music Publishing Australia). Lyrics reproduced with permission.
2. See 1 Kings 17:1–19:18.

Chapter 10 Being Spirit-filled Daily

1. J R W Stott (1987), *Baptism and Fullness*, InterVarsity, page 39.
2. R W Lyon, "Baptism and Spirit Baptism in the New Testament," *Westminster Theological Journal*, Vol 14 (Spring, 1979), page 1.
3. Stott, op cit, pages 61–62.
4. ibid, page 50.
5. See also G F Williams (1991), *How to be Filled with the Holy Spirit and Know It*, Review and Herald, pages 80–85.
6. Stott, op cit, page 59.
7. ibid, page 57.

Empowered: Enjoy His Presence

1. K Galliott (2020), "From the Editor," *Spirit of Australia: Qantas* (In-flight magazine), (February).
2. A Jorgensen (1987), "Someone Else to Stand by You," *Record*, November 7, pages 4–5, quoting Ellen White, *Steps to Christ*, page 125.
3. Ellen White (1892), *Steps to Christ*, Pacific Press Publishing Association, pages 74.
4. The verb for "breathe" used in this verse is not used elsewhere in the New Testament, but at creation, God "breathed the breath of life into the man's nostrils, and the man became a living person" (Genesis 2:7).
5. For further comment, see Ellen White (1898), *The Desire of Ages*, Pacific Press Publishing Association, page 823; Ellen White (1905), *The Ministry of Healing*, Pacific Press Publishing Association, page 226.
6. R Warren (1995), *The Purpose Driven Church*, Zondervan, page 13.
7. P Roennfeldt (2018), *If You Can Eat, You Can Make Disciples*, Signs Publishing, page 8.
8. ibid.
9. See P Roennfeldt (2017), *Following Jesus*, Signs Publishing;
   P Roennfeldt (2018), *Following the Spirit*, Signs Publishing;
   P Roennfeldt (2019), *Following the Apostles' Vision*, Signs Publishing.

Appendix C Second Blessing: The Merging of Perfectionism and Glossolalia

1. D L Burnett (2006), *In the Shadow of Aldersgate: An Introduction to the Heritage and Faith of the Wesleyan Tradition*, Wipf and Stock Publishers, pages 116–117. Burnett writes, "The concept of entire sanctification is so pervasive throughout church history that it can accurately be said that virtually all the major traditions—Orthodox, Catholic, Reformed, and Anglican—played some part in shaping Wesley's passion for holiness."
2. J Wesley (1777), *A Plain Account of Christian Perfection*, <en.wikisource.org/wiki/A_Plain_Account_of_Christian_Perfection>.
3. J Williams (2010), *Religion and Violence in Early American Methodism: Taking the Kingdom by Force*, Indiana University Press, page 150.
4. T A Campbell (1996), *Christian Confessions: A Historical Introduction*, Westminster John Knox Press, page 237.
5. D Pawson (1988), *Fourth Waves*, Hodder and Stoughton, pages 51–52.

6. J Barna, "Adventism and Biblical Perfection," pages 5–6, <www.academia.edu/15308673/Adventism_and_Biblical_Perfection_The_Diverse_Roots_of_Perfectionist_Thinking_in_Adventism_and_the_Need_for_Biblical_Definition_of_Perfection>.
7. A L White (editor), *Charismatic Experiences in Early Seventh-day Adventist History*, Ellen G White Estate.
8. R J Foster (1998), *Streams of Living Water: Celebrating the Great Traditions of the Christian Faith*, HarperCollins, pages 118–122.
9. ibid, pages 122–125.
10. Pawson, op cit, pages 55–61.
11. ibid, pages 59–61; see also N R Gulley (1995), "Biblical Evaluation of the Charismatic 'Second Blessing,'" in *The Ministry of the Holy Spirit* (Record Supplement), (editor G Pflandl), pages 21–25, South Pacific Division of Seventh-day Adventists.

ACKNOWLEDGMENTS

While written recently, this book has been prepared over many decades. The Holy Spirit, in particular His baptism and filling, has been a focus of my study and reflection, and the theme of my teaching and preaching in many countries—in local churches, discipleship conferences, church-planting exchanges, youth retreats, camp-meetings and conventions, pastors' and evangelistic meetings. I want to express gratitude to every person who has enriched my relationship with the Spirit though their insights and prayers.

And I thank friends and colleagues who have encouraged the writing of this book:

Thanks to Leigh Rice, Christina Hawkins, Nick Kross and Wayne Krause—of the South Pacific Discipleship Ministries Team—for their special interest in this theme and their persistent encouragement.

Thanks to Alina and Martin van Rensburg, Young Adult Ministry Leaders in Queensland, for their enthusiastic encouragement.

Thanks to Wayne Piez, a medical doctor and Christian leader, for his keen insights, each of which provoked a tweaking of expression to ensure biblical, ethical and practical balance.

Thanks to my brother, Ray Roennfeldt, pastor, systematic theologian and former Vice-Chancellor of Avondale University College (2009–2020), for helpful insights regarding the holiness-charismatic streams within Methodism and early Adventism.

Thanks to Kevin Giles, Anglican pastor, theologian, author and friend, for giving careful attention to ensure my writing reflects true biblical Trinitarian understanding.

Thanks to Darren Slade, pastor and denominational administrator—with whom I have spent weeks at a time visiting churches across northern Queensland and the Northern Territory—for his attention to both the details and big picture. He provided many helpful ideas to give life and clarity to this book.

Thanks to John Denne, pastor and colleague, for his suggestions, including ensuring that Paul's imperative for believers to "go on being filled" with the Spirit be emphasised.

Thanks to Lea-Anne Smith, a Christian bookshop manager and research student, whose work exploring the impact of the 20th-century tongues-movement provided important insights to clarify my writing.

Thanks to Reinder Bruinsma, Adventist pastor, missiologist, historian, denominational leader, author and colleague, for his encouragement and helpful suggestions in shaping this work.

Thanks to Terry Johnson, pastor and denominational administrator, for reading this book during his "own personal revival in experiencing the Spirit's daily filling"—and for urging all to experience the Spirit's filling to meet our greatest needs as believers and the church.

Thanks again to Stephan Herzog, international business consultant, for checking every line of an early draft, noting adjustments needed and—together with Tony Robinson, Jon Amiss and Len Farquharson (our men's group)—for his enthusiastic encouragement.

Thanks to Rex Edwards, former Griggs University Vice-President of Religious Studies and Assistant Director of Research, General Conference Biblical Research Institute, pastor-to-pastors, mentor and friend, who shared countless early morning devotional times with me, during teaching and evangelistic assignments in many countries, reading together some of the classics on Holy Spirit baptism.

Thanks to Maureen Barnes, my former secretary (of some years ago!) for willingly and voluntarily proofreading the whole manuscript, as well as raising many questions and sharing valuable comments.

Thanks to each of my sibling—sisters Lyn (Anderson) and Julia (Chapman), Phil and Ray—for ensuring the accuracy of memories of people and places from our earlier years.

Thanks to my book editors Nathan Brown and Lauren Webb, whose wide interests and experience, together with their editorial expertise, gracious persistence and commitment have refined my writing. While I take responsibility for the content, I thank Nathan, Lauren and all the Signs Publishing team for their work, encouragement and support in preparing my books. I value and appreciate them all, for their dedication and hard work. Special thanks to Shane Winfield for the cover designs.

Very special thanks to Judy for her patience, wisdom and practical expressions of faith. For almost 50 years of marriage and ministry, she has been a testimony to the Spirit's filling and empowering as a caring, helpful and generous neighbour, friend, Mum and Grandma.

And above all, I thank the Spirit. He "who raised Jesus from the dead" now lives within, and He "speaks to us deep in our hearts [telling] us that we are God's children" (Romans 8:11, 16). Thank You, Holy Spirit.

Peter Roennfeldt

peter@newchurchlife.com

PETER ROENNFELDT

IF YOU CAN EAT . . . YOU CAN MAKE DISCIPLES

SHARING FAITH IN A MULTI-FAITH WORLD

"God's heart for all people is on every page. Read this book, then live it. That's where the joy is!"
—*Kayle de Waal, head of Avondale Seminary, author,* Mission Shift